Foreword

In the field of psychology we believe that the student ought to get the "feel" of experimentation by reading original source materials. In this way he can acquire a better understanding of the discipline by seeing scientific ideas grow and change. However, one of the main problems in teaching is the limited availability of these sources, which communicate most effectively the personality of the author and the excitement of ongoing research.

For these reasons we have decided to edit several books,* each devoted to a particular problem in psychology. In every case we attempt to select problems that have been and are controversial—that have been and still are alive. We intend to present these problems as a set of selected original articles which are arranged in historical order and in order of progress in the field. We believe that it is important for the student to see that theories and researches build on what has gone before; that one study leads to another, that theory leads to research and then to revision of theory. We believe that *telling* the student this does not make the same kind of impression as letting him see it happen in actuality. This is the rationale behind this series of problems books. Editor's remarks are kept to the absolute minimum. The idea is for the student to read and build ideas for himself. (It should also be pointed out that articles deemed too technical are not included.)

Suggestions for Use

These readings books can be used by the student in either of two ways. They are organized so that, with the help of the instructor (or of the students if used in seminars), a topic can be covered at length and in depth. This would necessitate lectures or discussions on articles

* (Pub. note: to be a sub-series within the Insight Book Series)

not covered in the series to fill in the gaps. On the other hand, each book taken alone will give a student a good idea of the problem being covered and its historical background as well as its present state and the direction it seems to be taking. At the risk of being repetitious, we would like to say again that we believe it is important for the student to see how theories and researches lead to other researches and revision of theories. It is also important for the student to become familiar with significant researches at first hand. It is to these ideas that this sub-series on enduring problems in psychology is dedicated.

Amherst, Mass. R.C.B.
Lewisburg, Pa. R.C.T.
January, 1961

Contents

PART IV

PART V

Introduction

Any effort to bring together a limited set of readings on the topic of reinforcement immediately encounters a number of difficulties. First, there is the definition of the term to consider. At least five basic definitions are currently employed, and they are by no means closely related. Second, the term is used by two major approaches to the study of learning which, despite occasional indications of mutual awareness, have tended to push along independently. We refer here, of course, to the drive reductionists and the associationists.

This volume attempts to provide the reader with a view of the work done by the drive reductionists and their devoted critics. Beginning with Thorndike's postulation of the law of effect we see the progressive elaboration of the term "effect" in the writings of Hull, and subsequently the reworking of Hull's definition by Miller and Dollard. The portion of Guthrie's writing presented is given to provide sharp contrast with Hull's position. Part II of the readings introduces the earliest and most persistent types of researches designed to put the drive reduction notion of reinforcement to the test. These "latent learning" studies and their interpretation stirred up a good deal of controversy.

Part III contains only one article. In this section, Mowrer, initially committed to the utility of the drive reduction hypothesis, chooses to supplement it with the postulation of a two-factor theory of learning which he feels can handle data not easily explicable by either of the factors alone.

The last portion contains recent studies which raised increasingly sharp questions concerning the operational definition to be given the terms "effect" or "reduction." Sheffield and his students are represented by a paper which describes unmistakable learning in the absence of any plausible drive or stimulus reduction. Miller and his students take up this challenge and attempt to show that operational localization of such effects can be demonstrated. Finally, the Olds and Milner article is included as a recent break with the methods of the past which has the effect of suggesting new ways to talk about the problem of response consequence effects on response acquisition. Miller's summary refers to the wide body of research on the learning process and traces the utility and shortcomings of the "reduction" definition of the law of effect.

Earlier mention was made of the work of the associationists in the field of learning research. These workers, beginning with Pavlov and represented through the years by Guthrie and Skinner, also use the term reinforcement but do so in a descriptive way devoid of further implication of effect on the organism. By refusing to consider this possibility they have been free to concentrate on systematic exploration of certain situational parameters as they affect response acquisition. It was our feeling that these studies lay outside the scope of this volume; perhaps a separate volume for them is justified.

It seems quite likely that a topic such as reinforcement has been sufficiently overworked to produce considerable disagreement about which studies are the most important. Judging from the tenor of many of the articles considered for this book, it is a certainty that far more partisan selections might have been made for one disposition or another. However, this volume attempts to keep the uncommitted reader in mind, and assumes that he is quite capable of pursuing any topic that stimulates him to seek additional materials.

Part I

1

Provisional Laws of Acquired Behavior or Learning

E. L. Thorndike

The Law of Effect is that: *Of several responses made to the same situation, those which are accompanied or closely followed by satisfaction to the animal will, other things being equal, be more firmly connected with the situation, so that, when it recurs, they will be more likely to recur; those which are accompanied or closely followed by discomfort to the animal will, other things being equal, have their connections with that situation weakened, so that, when it recurs, they will be less likely to occur. The greater the satisfaction or discomfort, the greater the strengthening or weakening of the bond.*

The Law of Exercise is that: *Any response to a situation will, other things being equal, be more strongly connected with the situation in proportion to the number of times it has been connected with that situation and to the average vigor and duration of the connections.*

These two laws stand out clearly in every series of experiments on animal learning and in the entire history of the management of human affairs. They give an account

---

In 1911 E. L. Thorndike published his book *Animal Intelligence* (New York, The Macmillan Company). The book presents a considerable body of information obtained from laboratory studies dealing with learning in the cat, rat, and humans. The emphasis of these studies is upon the identification and isolation of the conditions which influence the speed, and retention of various types of learning materials. In the section presented here Thorndike turns to the formulation of general laws which are inductively determined from a consideration of the laboratory data. The following selection is from Chapter VI pp. 241-250 of Animal Intelligence.

of learning that is satisfactory over a wide range of experience, so long as all that is demanded is a rough and general means of prophecy. We can, as a rule, get an animal to learn a given accomplishment by getting him to accomplish it, rewarding him when he does, and punishing him when he does not; or, if reward or punishment are kept indifferent, by getting him to accomplish it much oftener than he does any other response to the situation in question.

For more detailed and perfect prophecy, the phrases 'result in satisfaction' and 'result in discomfort' need further definition, and the other things that are to be equal need comment.

By a satisfying state of affairs is meant one which the animal does nothing to avoid, often doing such things as attain and preserve it. By a discomforting or annoying state of affairs is meant one which the animal commonly avoids and abandons.

The satisfiers for any animal in any given condition cannot be determined with precision and surety save by observation. Food when hungry, society when lonesome, sleep when fatigued, relief from pain, are samples of the common occurrence that what favors the life of the species satisfies its individual members. But this does not furnish a completely valid rule.

The satisfying and annoying are not synonymous with favorable and unfavorable to the life of either the individual or the species. Many animals are satisfied by deleterious conditions. Excitement, overeating, and alcoholic intoxication are, for instance, three very common and very potent satisfiers of man. Conditions useful to the life of the species in moderation are often satisfying far beyond their useful point: many conditions of great utility to the life of the species do not satisfy and may even annoy its members.

The annoyers for any animal follow the rough rule that alterations of the animal's 'natural' or 'normal' structure—as by cuts, bruises, blows, and the like,—and deprivations of or interference with its 'natural' or 'normal' activities,—as by capture, starvation, solitude, or indigestion,—are intolerable. But interference with the structure and functions by which the species is perpetuated is not a sufficient criterion for discomfort. Nature's adaptations are too crude.

Upon examination it appears that the pernicious states of affairs which an animal welcomes are not pernicious *at the time, to the neurones*. We learn many bad habits, such as morphinism, because there is incomplete adaptation of all the interests of the body-state to the temporary interest of its ruling class, the neurones. So also the unsatisfying goods are not goods to the neurones at the time. We neglect many benefits because the neurones choose their immediate advantage. The neurones must be tricked into permitting the animal to take exercise when freezing or quinine when in a fever, or to free the stomach from certain poisons.

Satisfaction and discomfort, welcoming and avoiding, thus seem to be related to the maintenance and hindrance of the life processes of the neurones rather than of the animal as a whole, and to temporary rather than permanent maintenance and hindrance.

The chief life processes of a neurone concerned in learning are absorption of food, excretion of waste, reception and conduction of the nerve impulse, and modifiability or change of connections. Of these only the latter demands comment.

The connections formed between situation and response are represented by connections between neurones and neurones, whereby the disturbance or neural current arising in the former is conducted to the latter across their synapses. The strength or weakness of a connection means the greater or less likelihood that the same current will be conducted from the former to the latter rather than to some other place. The strength or weakness of the connection is a condition of the synapse. What condition of the synapse it is remains a matter for hypothesis. Close connection might mean protoplasmic union, or proximity of the neurones in space, or a greater permeability of a membrane, or a lowered electrical resistance, or a favorable chemical condition of some other sort. Let us call this undefined condition which parallels the strength of a connection between situation and response the intimacy of the synapse. Then the modifiability or connection changing of a neurone equals its power to alter the intimacy of its synapses.

As a provisional hypothesis to account for what satisfies and what annoys an animal, I suggest the following:—

A neurone modifies the intimacy of its synapses so as to keep intimate those by whose intimacy its other life processes are favored and to weaken the intimacy of those whereby its other life processes are hindered. The animal's action-system as a whole consequently does nothing to avoid that response whereby the life processes of the neurones other than connection-changing are maintained, but does cease those responses whereby such life processes of the neurones are hindered.

This hypothesis has two important consequences. First: Learning by the law of effect is then more fully adaptive for the neurones in the changing intimacy of whose synapses learning consists, than for the animal as a whole. It is adaptive for the animal as a whole only in so far as his organization makes the neurones concerned in the learning welcome states of affairs that are favorable to his life and that of his species and reject those that are harmful.

Second: a mechanism in the neurones gives results in the behavior of the animal as a whole that seem beyond mechanism. By their unmodifiable abandonment of certain specific conditions and retention of others, the animal as a whole can modify its behavior. Their one rule of conduct causes in him a countless complexity of habits. The learning of an animal is an instinct of its neurones.

I have limited the discussion to animals in whom the connection-system is a differentiated organ, the neurones. In so far as the law of effect operates in an animal whose connection-system is not anatomically distinguishable and is favored and hindered in its life by the same conditions that favor and hinder the life of the animal as a whole, the satisfying and annoying will be those states of affairs which the connection-system, whatever it be, maintains and abandons.

The other things that have to be equal in the case of

the law of effect are: First, the frequency, energy and duration of the connection,—that is, the action of the law of exercise; second, the closeness with which the satisfaction is associated with the response; and, third, the readiness of the response to be connected with the situation.

The first of these accessory conditions requires no comment. A slightly satisfying or indifferent response made often may win a closer connection than a more satisfying response made only rarely.

The second is most clearly seen in the effect of increasing the interval between the response and the satisfaction or discomfort. Such an increase diminishes the rate of learning. If, for example, four boxes were arranged so that turning a button caused a door to open (and permit a cat to get freedom and food) in one, five, fifty and five hundred seconds, respectively, a cat would form the habit of prompt escape from the first box most rapidly and would almost certainly never form that habit in the case of the fourth. The electric shock administered just as an animal starts on the wrong path or touches the wrong mechanism, is potent, but the same punishment administered ten or twenty seconds after an act will have little or no effect upon that act.

Close temporal sequence is not the only means of insuring the connection of the satisfaction with the response producing it. What is called attention to the response counts also. If a cat pushes a button around with its nose, while its main occupation, the act to which its general 'set' impels it, to which, we say, it is chiefly attentive, is that of clawing at an opening, it will be less aided in the formation of the habit than if it had been chiefly concerned in what its nose was doing. The successful response is as a rule only a part of all that the animal is doing at the time. In proportion as it is an eminent, emphatic part of it, learning is aided. Similarly discomfort eliminates most the eminent, emphatic features of the total response which it accompanies or shortly follows.

The third factor, the susceptibility of the response and situation to connection, is harder to illustrate. But, apparently, of those responses which are equally strongly connected with a situation by nature and equally attended to, some are more susceptible than others to a more intimate connection.

The things which have to be equal in the case of the law of exercise are the force of satisfyingness; that is, the action of the law of effect, and again the readiness of the response to be connected with the situation.

2

The Acquisition of Receptor-Effector Connections—Primary Reinforcement

C. L. Hull

We have seen above that organisms require a considerable variety of optimal conditions if the individual and the species are to survive. In many cases where the conditions, particularly internal ones, deviate materially from the optimum, complex automatic physiological processes make the adjustment. An example of this is the remarkable manner in which the blood is maintained at a practically constant state in the face of a great variety of adverse conditions. This type of automaticity has been called by Cannon the "wisdom of the body." In the case of certain other needs, and here lies our chief interest, the situation is remediable only by movement, i.e., muscular activity, on the part of the organism concerned. The processes of organic evolution have produced a form of nervous system in the higher organisms which, under the conditions of the several needs of this type, will evoke without previous learning a considerable variety of movements each of which has a certain prob-

---

Clark Hull's publications on learning theory began in the early thirties. Working with his students at Yale, he was able to test, revise, and re-test various formal statements of his theory. By 1943 his *Principles of Behavior* was ready for publication; a major revision of it appeared in 1952. The bulk of his book is concerned with variables affecting habit strength, and the effect of the latter on performance. The selection presented below is confined to the central postulate of the role played by need reduction in the production of increased increments in habit strengh. (*From Principles of Behavior* by Clark L. Hull. Copyright 1943, D. Appleton-Century Co., Inc. Reprinted by permission of Appleton-Century-Crofts, Inc.)

ability of terminating the need. This kind of activity we call *behavior*.

THE PROBLEM AND GENERAL NATURE OF LEARNING

It is evident, however, that such an arrangement of ready-made (inherited) receptor-effector tendencies, even when those evoked by each state of need are distinctly varied, will hardly be optimally effective for the survival of organisms living in a complex, highly variable, and consequently unpredictable environment. For the optimal probability of survival of such organisms, inherited behavior tendencies must be supplemented by learning. That learning does in fact greatly improve the adaptive quality of the behavior of higher organisms is attested by the most casual observation. But the detailed nature of the learning process is not revealed by casual observation; this becomes evident only through the study of many carefully designed and executed experiments.

The essential nature of the learning process may, however, be stated quite simply. Just as the inherited equipment of reaction tendencies consists of receptor-effector connections, so the process of learning consists in the strengthening of certain of these connections as contrasted with others, or in the setting up of quite new connections. In many ways this is the highest and most significant phenomenon produced by the processes of organic evolution. It will be our fascinating task in the present and several succeeding chapters to tease out bit by bit from the results of very many experiments the more important molar laws or rules according to which this supremely important biological process takes place.

In accordance with the objective approach outlined in Chapter II we must regard the processes of learning as wholly automatic. By this it is meant that the learning must result from the mere interaction between the organism, including its equipment of action tendencies at the moment, and its environment, internal as well as external. Moreover, the molar laws or rules according to which this interaction results in the formation or strengthening of receptor-effector connections must be capable of clear and explicit statement. Recourse cannot be had to any monitor, entelechy, mind, or spirit hidden within the organism who will tell the nervous system which receptor-effector connection to strengthen or which receptor-effector combination to connect *de novo.* Such a procedure, however it may be disguised, merely raises the question of the rule according to which the entelechy or spirit itself operates; this, of course, is the original question all over again and clarifies nothing.

THE STRENGTHENING OF INNATE RECEPTOR-EFFECTOR CONNECTIONS

Because of its presumptive temporal priority in the life of the organism, we shall consider first the problem of the selective strengthening of one among a variety of inherited movement tendencies evoked by a need in a particular environing situation. This can perhaps best be done by means of an illustrative experiment, even though some of the reaction tendencies there operative may already have been modified by learning. The experimental procedure and the results will be described in a little detail, out of consideration for readers who have slight knowledge of the routine methodologies characteristic of behavior laboratories.

Demonstration Experiment A. The laboratory in which the experiment is performed is without windows and its walls are painted black; this gives the room an appearance of being rather dimly illuminated, though in fact it is not. On a table rests a black wooden apparatus about two feet long, a foot wide, and a foot high. It has a hinged glass lid which permits clear observation of the interior. The floor of the box consists of small transverse rods of stainless steel placed about a quarter inch apart. Midway between the two ends of the box is a partition consisting of the same type of metal rods similarly arranged but placed vertically. This partition or barrier reaches to within about four inches of the lid. A two-throw electric switch permits the charging of the floor rods of either compartment and of the partition with a weak alternating current.

On a second table nearby there rests a wire cage containing a sleek and lively albino rat about one hundred days of age. The laboratory technician opens the lid of the cage and the rat at once stands up on its hind legs with its head and forepaws outside the aperture. The technician grasps the rat about the middle with his bare hand and transfers it to one of the compartments of the apparatus. The animal, after a brief pause, begins moving about the compartment, sniffing and inspecting the various parts, often stretching up on its hind legs to its full length against the walls of the box.

After some minutes the technician throws the switch which charges both the partition and the grid upon which the rat is standing. The animal's behavior changes at once; in place of the deliberate exploratory movements it now displays an exaggeratedly mincing mode of locomotion about the compartment interspersed with occasional slight squeaks, biting of the bars which are shocking its feet, defecation, urination, and leaps up the walls. These reactions are repeated in various orders and in various parts of the compartment; sometimes the same act occurs several times in succession, sometimes not. After five or six minutes of this variable behavior one of the leaps carries the animal over the barrier upon the uncharged grid of the second compartment. Here after an interval of quiescence and heavy breathing the animal cautiously resumes exploratory behavior, much as in the first compartment. Ten minutes after the first leap of the barrier the second grid is charged and the animal goes through substantially the same type of variable behavior as before. This finally results in a second leaping of the barrier and ten minutes more of safety, after which this grid is again charged, and so on. In this way the animal is given fifteen trials, each terminated by a leap over the barrier.

A comparison of the animal's behavior leading to his successive escapes from the charged grid shows clear evidence of learning in that upon the whole the time from the onset of the shock to the escape became progressively less, until at the last few trials the leaping reaction followed the onset of the shock almost instantaneously.

Meanwhile the competing reactions gradually decreased in number until at the end they ceased to occur altogether. Once or twice the rat even leaped the barrier before the shock was turned on at all. Here, then, we have a clear case of *selective* learning.

It is evident from the foregoing that the final successful competition of the reaction of leaping the barrier (R_4) with the various futile reactions of the series such as leaping against the wooden walls of the apparatus (R_1), squeaking (R_2), and biting the floor bars (R_3) must have resulted, in part at least, from a differential strengthening of R_4. It is also evident that each of these competing reactions was originally evoked by the slightly injurious effects of the current on the animal's feet (the condition of need or drive, D) in conjunction with the stimulation (visual, cutaneous, etc.) arising from the apparatus at about the time that the reaction took place. The stimulation arising from the apparatus at the time of the respective reactions needs to be designated specifically: leaping against the wall will be represented by S_A; squeaking, by $S_{A'}$; biting, by $S_{A''}$; and leaping the barrier, by $S_{A'''}$. It is assumed that preceding the learning, the leaping of the barrier was evoked by a compound connection between the receptor discharges s_D and s_A, arising from S_D and S_A respectively, and R_4; i.e., R_4 must have been evoked jointly by the converging connections, $s_D \longrightarrow R_4$ *and* $s_{A'''} \longrightarrow R_4$. These are the connections which evidently have been strengthened or reinforced. Because of this, learning is said to be a process of *reinforcement*.

We must now approach the central problem of learning by attempting to formulate the rule according to which primary reinforcement occurred in this case of selective learning. More specifically, we must ask the rule according to which the connections $\dot{s}_D \longrightarrow R_4$ and $\dot{s}_{A'''} \longrightarrow R_4$ were differentially strengthened so as to become dominant over the numerous other reaction tendencies. The most plausible statement of this rule at present available is: *Whenever a reaction* (R) *takes place in temporal contiguity with an afferent receptor impulse* ($\dot{s}$) *resulting from the impact upon a receptor of a stimulus energy* ($\dot{S}$), *and this conjunction is followed closely by* *the diminution in a need (and the associated diminution in the drive, D, and in the drive receptor discharge, s_D), there will result an increment, Δ ($\dot{s} \dashrightarrow R$), in the*

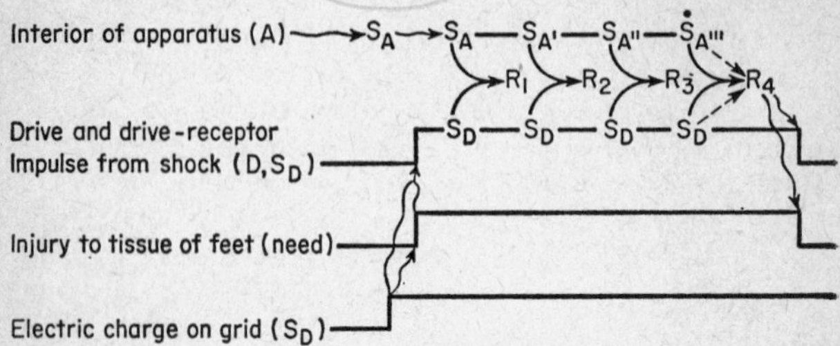

Fig. 1. Diagrammatic representation of the process of strengthening or reinforcing the connections between $s_D \rightarrow r_4$ *and* $s_{A'''} \rightarrow r$. *The step-like rises and falls of the several horizontal lines such as those of* D *and* s_D, *the shock to the tissue and* S_D, *represent the rise from zero and the fall of the respective processes. The arrows with wavy shafts (⇝) represent a physical causal relationship other than by way of receptor-effector stimulus evocation. Thus the rise of the current on the grid* (S_D) *causes the shock to the tissue of the animal's feet, the response of the receptor in the skin* (s_D) *of those regions, and the drive* (D) *or motivation to action. The separation of the foot from the grid by the act of jumping* (R_4) *terminates simultaneously the injurious action or need, the receptor discharge* (s_D), *and the drive* (D), *though the current on the grid remains unchanged. It is the reduction in the drive receptor impulse* (s_D) *and the drive* (D) *which are believed to be the critical factors in the process of reinforcement. The arrows with solid shafts (⟶), whether curved or straight, separate or jointed, represent receptor-effector relationships in existence before the learning process here represented occurred. The arrows with broken shafts (⇢) represent receptor-effector connections here in process of formation. Distance from left to right represents the passage of time.*

tendency for that stimulus on subsequent occasions to evoke that reaction. This is the "law" of primary reinforcement.[1]

[1] Actually, of course, this formulation has only the status of an hypothesis. The term *law* is here used in much the same loose way that Thorndike has used it in his famous expression,

Thus in the case of learning exhibited in Demonstration Experiment A, both of the afferent stimulus impulses, s_D and $s_{A'''}$, were obviously active when reaction R_4 occurred because they evoked it. Moreover, this conjunction of s_D and $s_{A'''}$ with R_4 was followed immediately by the termination of the shock effects or need, and so by a reduction in s_D. But by the principle of primary reinforcement just formulated this reduction in the need and drive (D) will, through the associated decrement in the drive receptor impulse (s_D), result in increments, Δ ($s_{A'''} \dashrightarrow R_4$) and Δ ($s_D \dashrightarrow R_4$), to the tendency for such conjoined afferent stimulus elements ($s_{A'''}$ and s_D) to evoke the reaction (R_4) on subsequent occasions. The major dynamic factors of this process are represented diagrammatically in Figure 1.

"law of effect," to which the above formulation is closely related.

3

Conditioning as a Principle of Learning

Edwin R. Guthrie

University of Washington

A theory of learning, to be effective, must account for the facts which have been established. The significance of the facts themselves is, unfortunately, not at present clear. Most experimental investigations have necessarily measured learning in terms of certain end results, however these were accomplished, leaving undetermined whether the subject has learned to do one thing in one way or one thing in many different ways. And most experimental investigations have concerned such intricate special activities that their results cannot be generalized. Theories of learning can attempt to systematize only the facts of the more elementary forms of learning.

Most of the facts of learning are derived from common knowledge. The elementary facts of learning were fairly well understood by the associationists. The role of experiment in this field is as a rule illustrative. Pavlov's 'conditioned reflex' is accepted because it fits into a body of common knowledge about human and animal nature. That burned children dread fires is accepted before hearing of Pavlov. If Pavlov's results had contradicted this body of common knowledge they would have been met with sceptical analysis. Even though they seem to corroborate common knowledge they deserve thorough examination.

This article originally appeared in the *Psychological Review*, 37, 1930, pp. 412-428.

I

The following paragraphs will serve to call to mind the more important and established facts of learning. The summary is necessarily incomplete because it will be restricted to such facts as are recognized by common consent.

1. *Conditioning.*—Stimuli which accompany a response tend, on their recurrence, to evoke that response. Sometimes called 'association by contiguity in time' or 'redintegration' or 'associative memory.' This generalization has long been recognized.

2. *Inhibitory Conditioning.*—Stimuli which tend to call out a response may lose that tendency, or, if they occur without the response, go further and acquire inhibiting effects. 'Negative adaptation' is the term proposed by Stevenson Smith and the writer a number of years ago for this characteristic of learning. The term 'conditioned inhibition' has also been used. 'Inhibitory conditioning' is perhaps better than either.

3. *Remote Conditioning.*—So little attention has been given to the precise time factors in conditioning that conditioning has generally been taken to include those cases in which the conditioning stimulus does not immediately precede its response, but may, an interval intervening, precede it or even follow it. According to Pavlov the interval in delayed and trace conditioning may be as great as thirty minutes. Pavlov would deny that the conditioning stimulus may follow its response, but studies in backward association would indicate that something resembling conditioning may occur in man when we have the time order, first response, then stimulus.

4. *Effects of Practice.*—Practice sometimes makes perfect. Repetition of a sequence of stimulus and response seems to establish the certainty of the sequence more firmly. 'Laws' of frequency or exercise are included in most theories of learning.

5. *Forgetting.*—The effects of learning seem to disappear, at a somewhat predictable rate. The 'curve of forgetting' discovered by Ebbinghaus for nonsense material applies with variations to many forms of learning, characterized by rapid disappearance at the interval just

following the last practice and a more gradual disappearance as time goes on. There are some odd exceptions to this general form of the curve, however. It is reported that the disappearance of learning is affected by intervening activity. After a period of sleep, retention is better than after a period of waking. After a period occupied in a quite different activity, retention is better than after a period in which the situation is like (but not too like) the situation during learning.

6. *Temporary Extinction.*—In direct contradiction to the preceding generalization, Dunlap and Pavlov have pointed out cases in which the repetition of a habit sequence serves to disrupt the habit. Dunlap reports the successful use of practice to break up annoying habits. Pavlov reports (and his report is well verified by common human experience) that conditioning will disappear if a conditioning stimulus is repeatedly given at short intervals without the support of the unconditioned stimulus. After an interval the habit will be found somewhat restored.

7. *Emotional Reinforcement.*—The familiar fact that learning is facilitated by states of general excitement has been illustrated by recent experiment showing that nonsense material is better learned by subjects under slight muscular strain than by relaxed subjects. We may associate this characteristic of learning with what has been called dynamogenesis, the facilitation of learning by adventitious stimuli which might well be expected to diminish learning.

8. *Irradiation.*—Lacking a better term we may use the one offered by the translator of Pavlov for a phenomenon which he describes and which is easily demonstrated for human behavior as well as for animal behavior. After a stimulus has been established as a conditioner of a response it may be found that other stimuli to the same class of receptors or, in some cases, to different receptors, are able to elicit the response, though they lacked this connection before the experiment. With a touch on the flank used in connection with acid as a stimulus for salivary secretion, touches on other parts of the body prove less effective as their distance from the flank is increased. With practice of the original combination

this conditioning power of neighboring stimuli tends to disappear.

9. *Patterns.*—Having learned to read, we find that reading appears to be more or less independent of the actual distance of the print from our eyes, and this means that similar patterns of stimuli are effective without reference to the particular receptor elements stimulated. The Gestalt psychologists assert that this response to patterns as such occurs without learning. It is here included as a characteristic of learning because the writer believes that it is dependent on learning. Reasons for this belief will be offered later.

10. *Insight.*—As in the case of reaction to patterns as such the Gestalt psychologists have pointed out that the higher animals and man occasionally meet a new situation with an adequate and new response. The process of trial and error, made so much of in recent behavioristic accounts of learning, seems to be omitted in many acts, which are characterized by the Gestalt psychologists as cases of insight. This fact is here listed among the characteristics of learning because it is also the author's belief that insight is dependent on learning. Reasons for this belief will be cited later.

The experimental literature suggests many more characteristics of learning. Most of these, however, are either debatable or are complicated with factors other than learning which make their significance for a theory of learning slight. The experiments on distribution of practice are complicated by fatigue. The results in whole and part learning are ambiguous and depend on the nature of the material. So-called 'reminiscence,' in which children prove to be able to reproduce more material after an interval than at the end of practice, has not so far been rid of the suspicion of continued unrecorded practice. A theory of learning which undertakes to explain all the suggested facts is apt to be caught predicting results which do not occur.

Is there a single formula which can be made to include all or most of the established generalizations concerning the nature of learning? If there is such a formula it will in all probability be some form of the ancient principle of association by contiguity in time, which has been a part of all theories of memory and learning since before Aristotle, and has retained its essential character in spite of a variety of names, such as 'conditioning,' 'associative memory,' 'redintegration.' The remainder of this paper will consider the possibility that the facts of learning may possibly all be cited as instances of simple conditioning.

In order to examine its possibilities, the principle of conditioning may be stated in a simple form: *Stimuli acting at a given instant tend to acquire some effectiveness toward the eliciting of concurrent responses, and this effectiveness tends to last indefinitely.*

The phrase 'tend to acquire' is used instead of 'acquire' because we have no assurance that this acquisition always occurs. It is the contention of this paper that this acquisition, when it does occur, is the fundamental mode of learning. The presumptive changes which make this re-routing of impulses lasting are the physiological basis of learning.

The principle is deliberately formulated to apply only to the momentary event. It is assumed that the phenomenon occurs during that small fraction of a second occupied by the conduction of an impulse through a center.

One more remark needs to be made concerning the language of the principle. The word 'stimuli' need not be taken in the sense of elementary stimuli to the individual receptor cells. It seems quite probable that patterns of such elementary stimuli may act as functional units and be subject to conditioning as units, that the elementary stimulus group *ABCD* may as a group excite a group of pathways *P*, while another stimulus group, *AEFG*, excites pathway *Q*. Conditioning redirection at remote association areas would affect these stimulus groups as functional units and not as elements. The stimulus *A* would be a conditioner of one response element through *P* and a conditioner of another, possibly an antagonistic element through the pathway *Q*.

The notion that such stimulus patterns might act as functional units *is not to be confused with the suggestion of the Gestalt psychologists that the patterns might act as functional units without reference to the receptors excited*. That is a very different matter.

We may now undertake an examination of the facts of learning in the light of this formulation of the ancient principle of association or conditioning. This amounts to an attempt to describe all of the forms of learning mentioned in the beginning as instances of the first, namely, simple, simultaneous conditioning. *This does not at all mean that learning is described in terms of conditioned reflexes*. This phrase assumes a fixed unit of behavior which is organized in stereotyped form. It tends to obscure the fact that the behavior of an intelligent organism at any instant is a resultant of the total stimulus situation including internal stimuli. Reflexes and responses are never twice alike, because the total stimulus situation is never repeated. We may, at the outset, distinguish a theory of learning in terms of *conditioning* from a theory of learning in terms of *conditioned reflexes*. We have made no assumptions concerning the elementary acts which comprise behavior.

II

The characteristics of learning mentioned at the beginning of the paper were: 1. Conditioning; 2. Inhibitory conditioning; 3. Remote conditioning; 4. Improvement by practice; 5. Forgetting; 6. Temporary extinction; 7. Emotional reinforcement; 8. Irradiation; 9. Response to pattern as such; 10. Insight. We may attack these in order.

1. *Conditioning*.—This is, of course, the principle itself, and hence needs no reduction. Our inquiry concerns the possibility of reducing the other facts of learning to instances of this. We may then begin with the second.

2. *Inhibitory Conditioning*.—The circumstances under which a stimulus combination which has previously elicited a response will lose the power to evoke that response may be briefly stated. If the stimulus combination occurs, and the response is prevented by any means, the stimulus combination loses its power to elicit the response and, if the situation is repeated, will acquire a

positive inhibiting effect on its former response. The response may have been prevented by inhibition from incompatible responses which prevail because the conditioning combination is weakened. Inhibitory conditioning is essentially the conditioning of inhibiting responses, and behaves like other conditioning in that it shows the effects of practice, is subject to forgetting, and so on.

3. *Remote Conditioning.*—In Pavlov's experiments a new stimulus is presented several seconds or minutes before an unconditioned stimulus, and then acquires the power to elicit the response unsupported, with a latent period corresponding to the interval used in the experiment. Pavlov's explanation attributes this delay to mysterious latencies in the nervous system. He supposes the impulse to be somehow 'held up' in the cortex. This assumption is quite unnecessary. Like Bechterev, Pavlov tends to forget that his experimental animals have sense organs which are stimulated by their own movements. When the bell rings, the dog responds by 'listening,' which is a series of movements, postural changes, turning of the head, pricking of the ears, and the like. When the salivary glands begin to secrete, the accompanying stimuli are not furnished by the bell but by these responses to the bell. The direct response to the bell is probably over in a small fraction of a second. After that the dog is responding to his first response to the bell. Just as when we answer the telephone we are, strictly speaking, answering the telephone only for an instant. After that we are answering ourselves, answering our start to answer the bell.

Such an explanation would account for a number of features of the 'delayed' and the 'trace' reflex. These are subject to inhibition or sudden release by new stimuli. What these new stimuli probably do is to alter the regular series of movements which comprise listening and the gradual recovery from listening. Delayed and trace reflexes are probably not direct conditioning at all. The true conditioning of saliva flow is on a stimulus pattern which follows the bell and is a consequence of the bell.

The apparent separation in time of a conditioning stimulus and its response is then quite possibly an illusion, and the assumption that responses to stimuli are either immediate or else do not occur at all is quite in accord with Pavlov's facts.

In delayed and trace reflexes the conditioning stimulus precedes the unconditioned. Pavlov states that no conditioning occurs if the stimulus to be made a conditioner follows the unconditioned stimulus. In a University of Washington experiment soon to be published something strongly resembling such 'backward' conditioning was found with human subjects. The results of experiments on backward association suggest this also. This form of remote conditioning may also be in reality based upon simultaneous conditioning. No acts are instantaneous. Contracted muscles, through their own sense organs, tend to maintain their contraction. A new stimulus which follows the stimulus for a particular act may easily be simultaneous with the proprioceptive stimulation involved in the act itself, and hence become a conditioner of the act.

4. *The Effects of Practice.*—Improvement as the result of practice is a familiar fact. The increased certainty of successful performance which results on repeated practice has led numerous psychologists to the notion that the attachment of a conditioning stimulus to its response is somehow increased by repetition of the sequence, which is a very different matter. Improvement demands more *detachment* of stimuli *from* responses than *attachment* of stimuli *to* responses. In order to improve in a performance the awkward, embarrassing, misdirected movements must be eliminated and replaced by movements which lead to a successful outcome. At the end of training the individual must be doing something quite different from what he was doing at the beginning of training.

The assumption that a stimulus-response sequence is made more certain by repetition has been embodied in a number of 'laws of exercise' or 'laws of frequency.' It is quite possible, however, that the assumption is a mistaken one.

Pavlov's results in experiments in conditioning seem at first glance to indicate unambiguously that a conditioning stimulus is 'established' by its repetition with a stimulus combination which elicits salivary flow, and to indicate that the 'strength' or certainty and lasting quality of its establishment is a function of the number of occasions on which the two stimuli have been paired.

These experiments may be given a quite different interpretation. Conditioning, so far as elementary conditioning stimuli are concerned, may be an all-or-nothing affair, analogous to the setting of a switch, and not analogous to the wearing of a path, which has been a favorite simile. The increased certainty of response following on a given stimulus situation may involve an increase in the number of conditioners, rather than an increased 'strength' of individual conditioners. In Pavlov's experiment, for instance, the bell signal results in extensive movements of orientation and postural adjustment, each movement causing appropriate stimulation to proprioceptors and exteroceptors. These movements are not identical each time the bell is struck because they depend in part on initial posture as well as on the bell. Repetition of the bell may enlist an increasing number of postural and other reflexes as conditioners of saliva flow, and hence gradually increase the certainty that salivary secretion will follow the bell.

It is entirely possible that if Pavlov could have controlled all stimuli instead of a very few, conditioning would be definitely established with one trial instead of fifty or more. The writer suggests that it is quite plausible that the more nearly such a complete control is established, the more nearly certain will be the result of the bell as a conditioner. Pavlov's whole method and experience suggest this.

The 'strengthening' of a stimulus-response connection with repetition may very possibly be the result of the enlistment of increasing numbers of stimuli as conditioners, and not the result of the 'strengthening' of individual connections.

5. *Forgetting.*—The conception of forgetting presented in the text-books has been that the effects of learning tend to be dissipated by some sort of physiological change at synapses which is a function of time. The form of the forgetting curve, though it differs for different sorts of material, indicates that forgetting is comparatively

rapid when practice is discontinued and that the rate regularly diminishes.

There are some signs of a shift of opinion toward an explanation of forgetting in terms of conditioning. Hunter, in his article on learning in the recent volume of 'The fundamentals of experimental psychology' quotes with approval the statement of Jenkins and Dallenbach in an article on 'Obliviscence during sleep and waking' that "the results of our study as a whole indicate that forgetting is not so much a matter of decay of old impressions and associations as it is a matter of interference, inhibition, or obliteration of the old by the new."

The evidence that forgetting is to be explained in terms of new conditioning is of several kinds. Forgetting is radically affected by intervening activities. If the intervening situations are materially different from the practice situations forgetting is less evident than when a certain amount of similarity holds of the situations. Probably the stimuli which are repeated while new responses prevail lose their conditioning effect on their previous responses and become conditioners of the new responses, and consequently inhibitors of the original ones. Furthermore, forgetting during a period of sleep is less than forgetting during a period of waking activity. This seems to be readily explained in the same terms. The stimuli which had become conditioners of certain responses are not repeated during sleep, and have no chance to be alienated from their attachment to these responses. During a period of waking, multitudes of stimuli from postural adjustments, movements, or from exteroceptive sources, which had been made conditioners of the activities in question are components of new situations and become conditioners of new responses. If we accept evidence from outside the laboratory we may quote those instances of vivid and detailed memories conserved for many years, which would, incidentally, have depended on one conditioning occasion rather than a practice series. The occasion for the restoration of such memories is probably an unusually complete restoration of situation, usually aided by such an absence of present distraction and inhibition as is found when we are on the border of sleep. Marcel Proust has described a common experience in which a memory evoked while lying in bed with closed eyes has persisted until a change in posture dissipated it completely. Association *may* occur after one connection, and *may* last indefinitely.

If forgetting is to be explained as new conditioning which replaces the old, how is the form of the curve of forgetting to be explained? Is it not entirely possible that the increased uncertainty of a conditioned response to a stimulus situation is due to the progressive alienation of conditioners from their response, an alienation explained by their acquisition of new allegiances? The curves of forgetting may owe their shapes to the cumulative effect of this alienation. Since the bulk of the conditioners are probably proprioceptive, the result of the organism's own movements, the activities following on a given case of conditioning would alienate whole regiments of conditioners at the start and a decreasing number as time elapsed, because there would be a decreasing number to eliminate.

This statistical decrease in conditioners with time which is described by the forgetting curve would resemble, to use a frivolous illustration, the decreased expenditures of a certain artist whose method of protecting himself from starvation was to change the proceeds of his rare sales into dimes and broadcast these about his large and disordered studio. The following day dimes were retrieved easily in numbers. As time went on more and more search was required, though he seldom reached such a pass that an afternoon's search would not yield a dime.

These last faithful dimes resemble the last faithful conditioners which are indicated by the failure of forgetting curves to reach the zero point. The fact that some forgetting occurs during sleep may be due to the fact that some activity occurs during sleep, and hence some chance for the alienation of stimuli.

This conception of forgetting explains forgetting entirely in terms of new conditioning. It is, of course, not denied that there may be physiological changes like those in senility which do result in the deterioration of memory, but the normal occasion of forgetting is the alienation of cues following the occurrence of these cues at times when their conditioned responses are excluded by the general situation.

6. *Temporary Extinction.*—Pavlov's temporary extinction and Dunlap's Beta law are also conceivable as instances of the general principle of conditioning. They might be described as forced forgetting.

When an established conditioner is repeated without the unconditioned stimulus, why should it quickly lose its conditioning power? Pavlov connects this loss with the brevity of the interval between applications. On his own showing this is not the determining factor. It is rather the *number of times the unsupported stimulus is repeated* that determines the extinction. Pavlov conceals this from himself by recording the results in terms of elapsed time from the start of the experiment. With short intervals, less elapsed time is required to extinguish, but in the case of both long and short intervals the number of applications is approximately the same.

If temporary extinction depends upon the number of times the conditioner is applied without support from the unconditioned stimulus, it is possible to explain temporary extinction in terms of the general principle of conditioning.

It should be noted, in the first place, that this temporary extinction or tendency to disappear with repetition is not an absolute generalization as it stands. It represents an exception to the rule of frequency. Sometimes one of these effects occurs, and sometimes the other. Obviously, in those cases in which temporary extinction prevails a special condition must have held. This special condition is probably what Pavlov asserts, the withdrawal of the unconditioned stimulus. It is the unconditioned stimulus that represents the most powerful determiner of the response. With the unconditioned stimulus withdrawn only occasional combinations of conditioners elicit the response, for it should be remembered that the animal is, in spite of sound-proof room and uniform lighting, in constant motion and subject to a continuously changing pattern of stimulation. At times there are more conditioners present, and at other times fewer. When the response fails, or is diminished because relatively few conditioners are present, these and other stimuli present become inhibitors, or, what is the same thing, conditioners of other responses.

There remains to be explained the reestablishment of the conditioned response after a lapse of time. We have a hint toward this explanation in the fact that a sudden extraneous and unusual stimulus may cause the conditioned response to recover its original strength and certainty. It is possible that the inhibiting stimuli in this case include the somewhat specific details of posture and environment which hold during the process of extinction. A sudden interruption disorganizes posture and orientation, removes many recently conditioned inhibitors, and allows the original posture and conditioners to prevail again. The reflex is restored much as a baulky horse is startled out of his baulking, or a man who has built up an obstinate attitude may be shaken out of it by a sudden change in situation.

7. *Emotional Reinforcement and Dynamogenesis.*—Explanation of the facilitating effect of exciting emotion on learning cannot be complete until a satisfactory physiology of the emotions has appeared. In the meantime attention may be called to the fact that exciting emotion involves general muscular tonus, and may possibly consist very largely in such increase in general tension. The physiologists have described many types of muscle-to-muscle reflexes which are excited by muscular contraction, the stretching of a muscle, or resistance to the contraction of a muscle. Intense stimulation of one receptor field resulting in the contraction of a limited number of muscles results in the contraction of other muscle groups through such muscle-to-muscle reflexes. States of general tension may be built up by the 'reverberation' of impulses in this fashion.

The origin of such states of general tension probably lies in intense stimulation of some receptor field, or in obstacles to free movement. In such states of general tension the acts which 'go through' are more energetic and complete. They involve the stimulation of many propriocepter systems which would be undisturbed by action not so energetic.

The increased stimulation would give opportunity for increased conditioners, especially since the excitement itself is subject to conditioned revival.

In what has been called 'dynamogenesis' we have possibly two ways in which the irrelevant stimuli may facilitate learning. The new stimuli may serve to increase general tonus through the 'reverberation' which has been described above and so serve to make action more vigorous and complete; and they may also, through the tendency to deflection which constitutes conditioning, serve to reinforce directly the prevailing responses.

8. *Irradiation.*—What Pavlov describes as irradiation, namely, the acquisition of conditioning effect by neighboring receptors which were not stimulated in training, may well be the result of simple conditioning, instead of the result of a direct spread of an entirely speculative condition with an inexplicable delay to neighboring portions of the projection areas of the cortex. It has already been suggested that the bell signal is not the direct conditioner in any of Pavlov's experiments, especially when it is learned that by 'simultaneous' presentation he usually means sounding the bell some two seconds before the food is presented. In two seconds many things may have happened. In direct response to the bell the dog 'listens.' The act of listening may be much the same whether the signal is a bell or a whistle of another pitch. Since the real conditioners of the salivary flow are the movements of listening, and not the bell, the whistle may result in salivary flow.

To a touch on the flank the dog responds by shifting his posture. This shift furnishes the conditioners of the glandular response. To a touch on a nearby point the response is a shift in posture involving much the same muscle groups as in the first case. To a touch on a more distant point the response will be different. The decreasing effect of stimulation of more remote areas may be the consequence of the decreasing likeness of the postural adjustment.

If we accept this much, Pavlov's experiments suggest the reason why 'irradiation' decreases with practice, since it is explained that with practice there is an increasing tendency for listening movements or defensive postural adjustments to disappear and give place to the eating movements and the eating posture.

One feature of these experiments as reported in 'Conditioned reflexes' remains unexplained. This is the statement that corresponding points on the two sides of the dog have exactly equal effect. Being unable to explain this, the writer may be forgiven for expressing some scepticism concerning the facts, which seem to have no analogue in human behavior.

9. *Patterns.*—That we do respond to patterns as such is not open to question. And this would seem to involve the complete breakdown of any theory of conditioning such as is being presented, for at varying distances the actual receptors and afferent paths activated by a visual pattern must be quite distinct. The fact, indeed, cannot be questioned, though it should be noted that it is not a general or uniform occurrence. The child who has learned to read the raised letters on his blocks will not ordinarily recognize the letters when he sits on them. The effectiveness of patterns applies only within very limited fields.

Is it not entirely possible that the method by which we come to recognize a face at different distances as that of one and the same person is essentially the same method by which we come to recognize the rear aspect of this same person as his own back? In this case of recognition there is no question of similar patterns, for the back of his head resembles his face less than his face resembles the faces of others. If we maintain an attitude, or repeat a response to an object while that object is the occasion of shifting stimulation and of new stimulus patterns the maintained response may be conditioned on the new stimuli. Our response to a person at different distances is the same, with differences appropriate to the distance. Why may we not attribute this sameness and this difference to the samenesses and the differences originally present in the stimuli furnished by our original behavior in his presence?

If we accept conditioning as an explanation for responding appropriately to a person on hearing his footstep, which offers a stimulation pattern quite different from the visual pattern to which we previously responded, why should we consider it mysterious that the appropriate response could be called out by the stimulation of a quite different group of visual receptors? The fact that they have the same pattern is irrelevant.

The Gestalt psychologists assert not only that we respond in similar ways to similar patterns, which we undoubtedly do, but also that we do this *without any opportunity for conditioning*, which the writer does not at all believe. In the case of the hen which performed its trick using the eye which had been blindfolded during learning, it is entirely possible that the cues for the proper movement were not primarily visual, but were furnished by movements connected with vision before the experiment was begun. Animals and man both have movements of skeletal muscles congenitally associated with vision. These movements may be in part identical for stimulation of either retina. If the act is conditioned on these movements, it might be elicited from either eye, without regard to which eye entered into practice.

10. *Insight.*—Concerning insight as described by the Gestalt psychologists, the writer has much the same opinion as concerning response to patterns. The facts which are reported are not to be questioned and are typical of the behavior of the higher animals. An important part of the report has, however, been omitted. If the behavior described as insight is asserted to occur without previous learning, the essential part of the experiment would be the control of previous learning, and in the experiments the histories of insight are conspicuously lacking. No new category of facts concerning learning has been shown to be offered by the behavior described as insight.

In the writer's experience, insight in animals and in man is the result of accumulated habit. It was not a strange coincidence that the most ingenious person ever at work in the local laboratory has been a practical engineer for many years. When this member of the staff solved with little hesitation problems which had baffled the writer, there was a choice of explanations. It could be said that one man had insight and the other none, which seemed the poorer explanation; or it could be pointed out that one man had had previous training and the other none, an explanation much more charitable.

SUMMARY AND COMMENTS

This paper has attempted to show that the main characteristics of learning, to wit, conditioning, inhibitory conditioning, remote conditioning, the effects of practice, forgetting, temporary extinction, emotional reinforcement, irradiation, response to patterns as such, and insight, may all be understood as instances of a very simple and very familiar principle, the ancient principle of association by contiguity in time. If the paper were not already too long many minor details which are readily described as instances of conditioning might be added. In their explanations of learning, Pavlov, the Gestalt psychologists, and many others have not examined sufficiently the possibilities of our proprioceptive sense organs in the role of determiners of behavior, and have tended to place the whole burden of explanation on highly speculative characteristics of the cerebral cortex.

This paper should be followed by some consideration of Lashley's work which appears to be at first sight a challenge to a general theory of conditioning. In the writer's opinion this work offers no objection whatever to the concept of conditioning. It does suggest that the simplest acts involve the stimulation of multitudes of receptors, the neglected proprioceptors among others, and the activation of multitudes of cortical pathways. As a simple example it might be suggested that what appears to be a visual discrimination may actually be conditioned upon movements which are reflex responses to visual stimulation through subcortical paths. But a proper consideration of Lashley's work would require many pages.

4

Reward

Neal E. Miller and John Dollard

Drive impels the person to make responses to cues in the stimulus situation. Whether these responses will be repeated depends on whether or not they are rewarded. If the response is non-rewarded, the tendency to repeat it to the same cues is weakened. Pavlov (1927) has called this process *extinction;* it will be discussed in more detail in the next chapter. In cases of sophisticated human learning, the process of extinction is facilitated by the learned habit of abandoning unsuccessful responses quickly. Thus in the experiment, the little girl went back to look under the same book only a few times and only on the first trial. The failure to see candy became a cue to abandon looking under that book.

As the dominant response is weakened by non-reward, the next response in the hierarchy becomes dominant. As successive responses are eliminated by non-reward, the individual exhibits variable or what has perhaps been misnamed *random behavior*. It is this variability that may lead to the production of a response which will be rewarded.

If one of the so-called random responses is followed by an event producing a reduction in the drive, the tendency to make this response on subsequent exposure to the same cues is increased. In other words, the connec-

---

The extension of Hullian theory to human learning, therapeutically produced changes in behavior and studies of personality development, is explored in *Social Learning and Imitation,* by Neal Miller and John Dollard (New Haven, Yale University Press, 1941, pp. 28-30). Their definition of drive, stimulus, and drive-stimulus reduction presents yet another way to approach the problem.

tion is strengthened between the stimulus pattern (drive and other cues) and the response. Events producing such strengthening are called rewards. A more technical name for reward is *reinforcement*. Relief from pain is a reward. Drinking water when thirsty, eating food when hungry, and relaxing when tired are other examples of primary, or innate, rewards.

If rewards are thought of as events producing a reduction in the drive, that is, in strength of stimulus, the relationship between satiation and reward becomes clear. Since it is impossible further to reduce the strength of a drive stimulus which is already zero, reward is impossible in the absence of drive. Thus, gulping food is no reward to a satiated animal and may even become painful so that regurgitation is rewarding.

If rewards produce reductions in drive, then too rapid repetition inevitably leads to satiation of the drive, with the result that the rewards lose their rewarding value until the drive reappears. In the absence of reward, the acts which have led to a previously rewarding event tend to be weakened through extinction. Such weakening is one of the factors which eventually cause responses appropriate to a given drive to cease in the absence of that drive. Did rewards not tend to weaken drives, there would be no mechanism for causing the individual to stop one line of satisfying behavior and turn to another.

Though it is convenient to think of rewards as events producing reductions in the strength of the drive stimulus, it is not necessary to be able to identify the drive which is reduced and the manner in which it is reduced in order to be able to determine empirically that certain events are rewards under certain circumstances and to make practical use of this information. Once it has been discovered that a given event, such as receiving praise from the mother, can be used as a reward to strengthen a given stimulus-response connection, e.g., the connection between the cue of a drippy feeling in the nose and the response of blowing the nose, it can be assumed that this same event can be used as a reward to strengthen other stimulus-response connections. Here the drive is probably some form of anxiety or desire to please the mother, but it is not absolutely essential to be able to identify the drive in order to discover that praise is a reward.

Any event known to strengthen stimulus-response connections may be called a reward. The term "reward" will be used hereinafter to refer to drive reduction, to events (such as eating when hungry) from which drive reduction may be reliably predicted, to the object (such as food) producing the drive reduction, and to other events empirically found to have the effect of strengthening cue-response connections. In the last instance, the definition is not circular so long as the fact that the event was found to strengthen one connection is used to predict that it will strengthen others.

Part II

5

The Effect of the Introduction of Reward upon the Maze Performance of Rats

Hugh Carlton Blodgett

PROBLEM

The purpose of this investigation was to study the efficiency of units of practice when unaccompanied by reward. The method devised was that of running two groups of rats through the maze: an *experimental group* which received no reward during the first part of learning, but which suddenly had reward introduced in the latter part of learning, and a *control group* which received reward throughout the whole of learning. The answer to the question as to the efficiency of non-reward units of practice was sought in a comparison of the learning curve of the experimental group (both before and after the introduction of reward) with that of the control group.

LITERATURE

Most of the previous experimental work on rewards and their relation to learning has been concerned with a comparison of the effectiveness of different incentives as such. The incentives have been sometimes different in quality as food and escape, and sometimes the same

---

This paper is an abridgment of a report entitled "The Relation of Reward to Animal Learning" submitted *in* partial fulfillment of the requirements for the Ph. D. degree in the Department of Psychology of the University of California and deposited in the Library of the University of California, May, 1925. It was originally published in The University of California Publications in Psychology, 1931, Vol. 4, pp. 113-134.

in quality, as two kinds of food, or two strengths of induction shock.

In addition to the general experiments indicating different strengths of reward without much attempt to analyze further what really may be involved, there are three experiments or parts of experiments strictly germane to our present study.

Lashley (1918), in a maze experiment upon distribution of practice, throws some light upon our problem. There were only 25 rats in all, divided into four groups: group A was allowed to run about in the maze for 20 minutes the day before the first run. During training, this group was given reward at the end of the run. Group B was a control, run once a day with the incentive of food; group C was run the same as A but was not allowed to correct errors; and group D was run with the incentive of food screened in the food box. The quickest learning was made by group A, the group which explored the maze for 20 minutes before the first run. The record of the control group, group B, was next best, group C was third, and group D, last.

Szymanski (1918) has published a series of articles upon the learning of maze habits with various kinds of reward. One of his experiments is closely related to our problem. Three rats were run through a maze to their home cage in which food had been placed. The rats were not hungry. At the end of 61 trials there was no reduction in time and error scores. Then the condition of experiment was changed so that the rats were run when they were hungry. They ran the maze perfectly in one or two trials.

Simmons (1924), in an article on relative effectiveness of various incentives, ran a group of 10 animals under conditions which she designated as delayed incentive. This group was run for five days without incentive. At the beginning and the end of the sixth trial, the animals were given a taste of food, such as was given the control group. In comparing the learning curves for this group and the control group, Simmons unfortunately combined the scores of her rats in groups of five days each. It is impossible, therefore, to determine the precise nature of the difference in the time and error scores for the two groups immediately after the incentive was given to the delayed-incentive group on the sixth day. This can be made clear by an analysis of the error curves given in her monograph.

As will be seen from the curve (fig. 1), the mean number of errors during the first five days, for the delayed group, was approximately 28 against an approximate 10 for the control group.

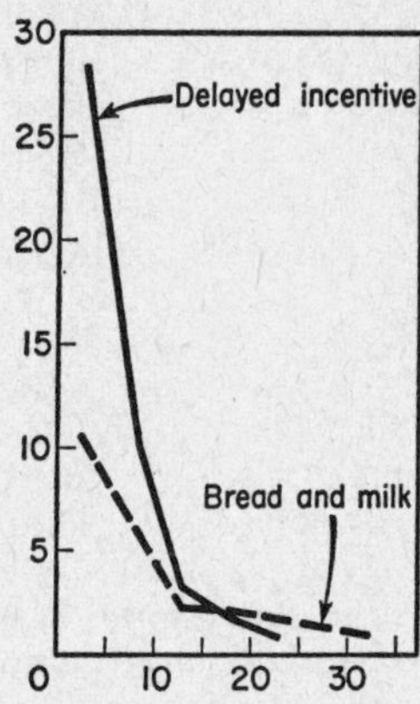

Fig. 1.

Day 6, which is averaged with four following days, was without incentive. As a result, the second point on the curve is a composite of the scores of one run which was made before incentive was introduced at the end of the run, and four runs which were made after the incentive had been introduced. Obviously this procedure masks any sudden change on the run following the first reward.

Simmons then compared the total number of trials required by the control group and by the delayed-incentive group to reach the learning criterion, the total number of errors for the groups, and the total amount of time. She found that the delayed-incentive group required fewer runs but that the error score and the time score were greater. This is because the errors and time scores made during the first six runs are figured in the total. She then made the same comparisons, leaving out the first five runs. Again she found the same results. This time, however, the superiority of the control group, in time and error scores, was less, because only one non-reward run (the sixth) was figured in the total. Finally, she compared trials, time, and errors, leaving out of account the first eight runs. In this case the delayed-incentive group reached the learning criterion in fewer trials, and made fewer errors and shorter times. This shows that a very marked change in time scores and error scores must have taken place in the delayed-incentive group between the fifth run and the eighth run. And one may assume that this change took place on the seventh run, after reward had been given at the end of the sixth run.

Attention should also be called to the fact that comparisons of scores for the latter part of the learning periods of the control group and the delayed-incentive group contain a spurious feature, namely, that practice for the two groups is not constant because of the much greater number of retracings made by the delayed incentive group during the non-reward period. And so the better final scores of the delayed-incentive group may be due to a different practice effect in the first six runs.

MATERIALS AND METHODS

Mazes.—Three mazes, A, B, and C, were used. Group plans are shown in figures 2, 3, and 4. Maze A and maze B had ordinary blinds. Maze C was a two-way maze presenting as alternatives a long and a short path to food.

All three mazes contained a feature not hitherto used in mazes. At each choice point, doors were installed which could be closed behind the animal. These doors were hinged at the top, and when open, lay along the top of the alley. They prevented retracings from one section of the maze to another, they were noiseless, and they caused no excitement in the animals. Their positions in the mazes are shown by the dotted lines, D. The value of this feature is fourfold: (1) it reduces the

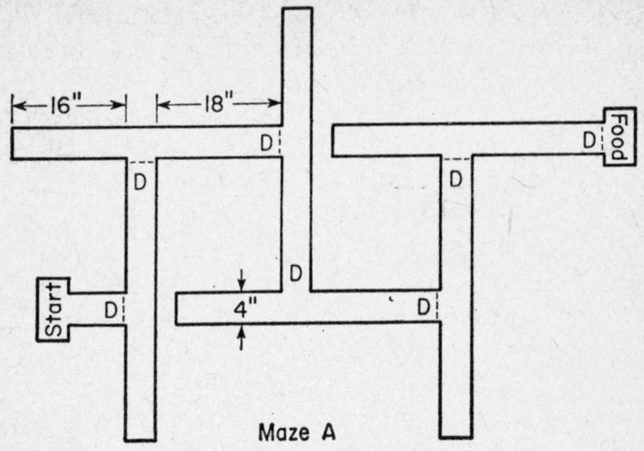

Fig. 2.

time of the experiment; (2) it standardizes each run by preventing the rat from running through the maze several times before entering the food box; (3) it equalizes practice in different parts of the maze; (4) it tends to cause a more symmetrical distribution curve of errors for a group of animals. For retracing tends, as such, to give some unduly large scores.

It may perhaps be argued that this introduction of doors was unsound because it introduced an artificial limit into the problem. Every experiment is necessarily artificial. Thus, for example, in the ordinary maze, the experimenter "artificially" excludes certain "normal" cues

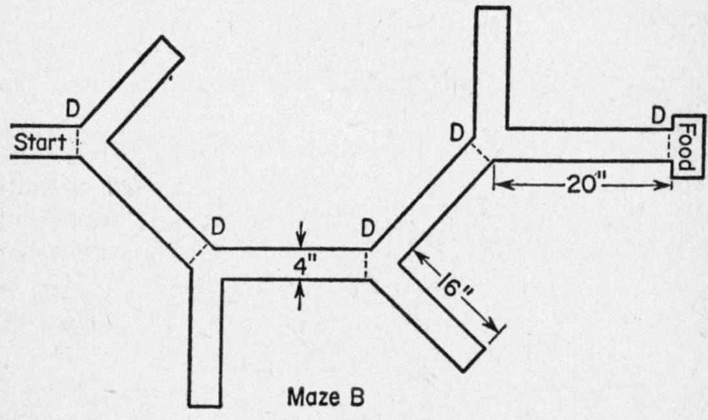

Fig. 3.

as, for example, odors and distinguishing tactful factors. All that has been done, in this case, is to restrict our conclusions to types of maze which do not allow retracings.

A second feature of importance which holds for mazes A and B is the fact that all the blind alleys in the same maze have the same dimensions and the same angular relationships to the true path. This is believed to be an improvement over the usual maze, in that the error scores (number of entrances into blinds) are more definitely scaled.

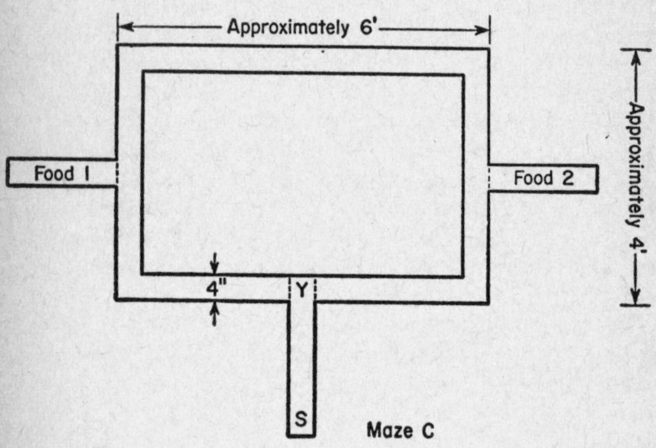

Fig. 4.

The mazes were constructed of wood painted dark brown. The walls were 8 inches high and ⅞ inch thick. The top of the alleys were covered with ¼ inch mesh wire screen. The alleys had no permanent bottom but were placed on a heavy piece of linoleum. The wire covers and the linoleum were painted the same color as the sides.

Animals.—The rats were of mixed strain, black and white. They were raised, four to six in a group, in wire cages 10 × 14 inches in a room varying in temperature from 55 to 85 degrees Fahrenheit. They were accustomed to occasional handling at feeding time and when their cages were cleaned, and so they were not wild. They were approximately three months of age when the experiment was begun. The number of males and females was nearly even.

Food.—Their food during the pre-experimental stage consisted of a mash of ground barley, bran, and table scraps. Beginning three days before the experiment and throughout the experimental period the animals were fed approximately one-tenth their weight of food saturated with water. They were given no other water. The food was a mixture of four parts dry bread, ground up in fine bits, one part bran, one part sunflower seed, and three-fourths part powdered skim milk.

Scoring.—With mazes A and B, a rat was counted as having made one error if it made one (or more) entrances of as much as a body's length (not counting tail) into a blind, while in a given segment of the maze. That is, even though the rat entered and re-entered a given blind before passing to the next segment, it was counted as having made only *one* error.

In maze C a rat was counted as having made one error whenever it took the long path rather than the short path to the food box.

Time was measured by a stopwatch, in seconds from the time the rat left the starting box until the door of the food box was closed behind it.

PROCEDURE AND RESULTS

Maze A: Groups I, II, and III

Group I. *Control.*—This group consisted of 36 rats run once a day for seven days and allowed to eat for *three minutes in the food box at the end of each run.* They were then removed to another cage (not the living-cage) and allowed to finish their day's ration, after which they were returned to their living-cages.

Group II. *Experimental.*—This group also consisted of 36 rats. (They were litter mates of group I. Of each original litter, half the number were put in group I, and half in group II.) *For the first six days,* group II found no food in the food box and were kept in it without reward for two minutes. They were then removed to another cage (not the living-cage) where they were fed after an interval of approximately one hour. Only then were they returned to their living-cages. *For day seven and the two subsequent days* they were treated exactly like group I; that is, they found food in the food box for three minutes and finished their day's ration immediately afterward in another cage.

Group III. *Experimental.*—This group consisted of 25 rats. Like group II, they began with no reward at

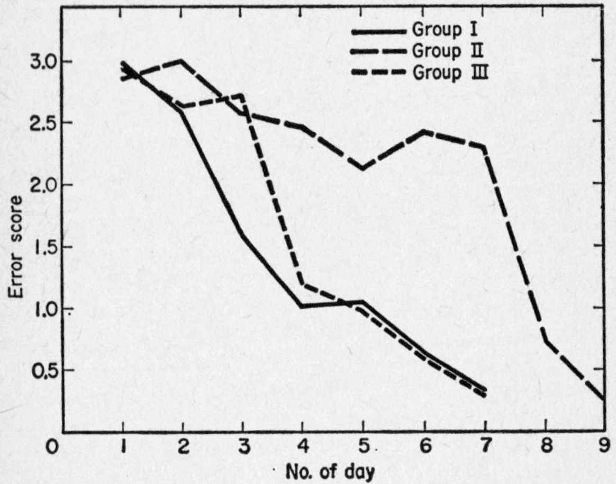

Fig. 5.

the end of the maze. But for them such reward was introduced at the end of the third day rather than at the end of the seventh day.

Figures 5 and 6 present the error curves and the time curves, for each of these groups. And tables 1 and 2 indicate the differences and the reliability of these differences between the three curves on each successive day.

Examining the error curves and tables, two points appear:

1. The experimental groups (II and III), so long as they were *without reward,* did very much worse than the

control group (I). In fact, the curves for groups II and III stayed almost horizontal until after the day (indicated by the cross) when food was introduced.

2. On the day after this first reward (i.e., on day 8 for group II and on day 4 for group III), errors dropped greatly. And on the second day after reward (i.e., on day 9 for group II and on day 5 for group III) the

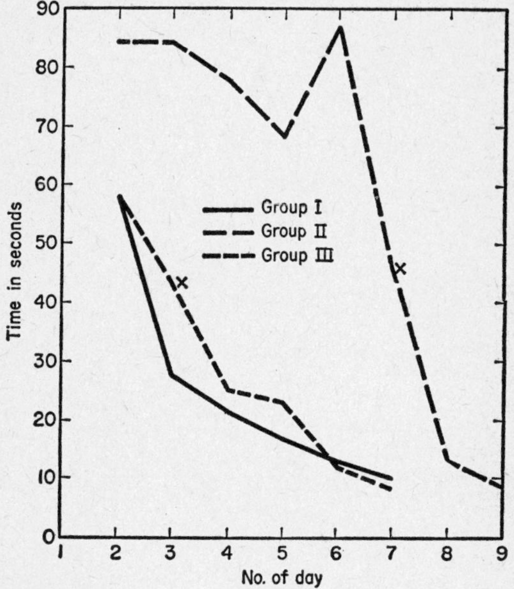

Fig. 6.

curves had dropped almost to the level of the curve for the control group.

Examining the time curves and tables, a similar picture appears, save that in the case of time the sudden drops seem to have come on the day of the introduction of the reward rather than on the day after. It appears, in other words, that although the rats had not yet, on that day, actually experienced the finding of the food, their times were shortened by the fact of its presence

TABLE 1

Mean errors

				GROUP II-GROUP I			GROUP III-GROUP I		
Day	Group I	Group II	Group III	Diff.	Diff.	Critical ratio	Diff.	Diff.	Critical ratio
1	2.97	2.89	2.96	−.08	.23	.35	−.01	.28	.04
2	2.56	3.03	2.64	.47	.28	1.66	.08	.30	.28
3	1.58	2.56	2.72	.97	.28	3.48	1.14	.27	4.27
4	1.03	2.47	1.20	1.44	.26	5.62	.17	.24	.71
5	1.08	2.08	.96	1.00	.24	4.26	.12	.30	.41
6	.69	2.42	.60	1.72	.28	6.17	.09	.20	.47
7	.30	2.28	.28	1.97	.20	12.72	.02	.13	.10
8	...	.86	...	...	...	...	...	...	...
9	...	.25	...	...	...	...	...	...	...

in the food box (though their errors, as has been seen, were not reduced). The explanation which suggests itself is that the odor of the food caused greater general activity and hence a shorter running time although it did not cause fewer errors. (For the rats had yet to learn *just where* the food was.)

A further question now arises. Do these sudden drops in errors which come after the introduction of reward indicate that something to be called a *latent learning* developed during the non-reward period—a latent learning which made itself manifest after the reward had been presented? Obviously, if this is to be answered in the

TABLE 2

Time (seconds)

				GROUP II-GROUP I			GROUP III-GROUP I		
Day	Group I	Group II	Group III	Diff.	Diff.	Critical ratio	Diff.	Diff.	Critical ratio
2	58.19	84.58	57.60	26.39	10.42	2.53	.59	7.38	.08
3	27.50	84.86	42.60	57.36	19.73	2.91	15.10	3.11	4.86
4	21.39	77.72	25.44	56.34	14.53	3.88	4.05	5.15	.79
5	16.22	67.64	23.32	51.42	8.54	6.02	7.10	5.07	1.40
6	13.06	87.22	12.76	73.97	19.20	3.85	.30	1.77	.17
7	9.97	46.70	8.84	36.72	4.04	9.09	1.13	1.07	1.06
8	...	12.46	...	...	...	...	...	...	...
9	...	8.61	...	...	...	...	...	...	...

affirmative, one must show that the drops which occurred immediately subsequent to the reward were larger than "normal," that is, that they were bigger than drops in the control curve.

The first way of checking this was to compare the drops made by group II between days 7 and 8 and by group III between days 3 and 4, with the largest drop made by group I between any two days which latter (see fig. 5) was obviously between days 2 and 3.

The results of this comparison are shown in table 3.

TABLE 3

Mean errors

	Drop in errors	Difference between drop and that shown in Group I	Difference	Critical ratio
Group I—Days 2-3	.972	...	...	...
Group II—Days 7-8	1.416	.444	.332	1.338
Group III—Days 3-4	1.520	.548	.355	1.544

The critical ratio of 1.338 when interpreted in terms of probability means that if there were no real difference between the drops shown by group II, days 7-8, and that shown by group I, days 2-3, a difference between these two drops as large as that obtained and shown in the table would occur by chance 904 times out of 10,000, or a little less than one-tenth of the time. It therefore seems probable, although not certain, that group II dropped more on this day than did group I (control) on the day of its greatest drop.

Similarly, the critical ratio of 1.544, when interpreted in terms of probability, means that, if there were no real difference between the drop shown by group III, days 3-4, and that shown by group I, days 2-3, a difference as large as that shown in the table would occur by chance 612 times out 10,000, or between one-fifteenth and one-sixteenth of the time. It again, therefore, seems probable, although not certain, that group III dropped more on this day than did group I on the day of its greatest drop.

Taking these two results together, the hypothesis that the periods of non-reward in groups II and III really produced *latent learning* which became manifest when a reward was introduced seems well supported.

A second way, however, of testing the validity of this hypothesis is suggested. It appears that it might be fair to compare the drops in group II and III not with the biggest actual drop made anywhere by group I, but rather with the interpolated drops made by group I from the *levels* corresponding to those from which the drops in groups II and III begin. In order to obtain these, an interpolative procedure was required. This (in the case of group II) was as follows: in figure 5 a horizontal was drawn to the left from the point of curve II corresponding to day 7, until this horizontal intersected curve I. A vertical was then dropped from this intersection to the X-axis. And a distance was thence measured off to the right, equal to the unit of one day. Another vertical was erected from this new point until curve I was again intersected, and the vertical distance between the two intersections on curve I was taken as the demanded drop. A similar procedure was followed with respect to group III.

Finally, however, in order to compare these interpolated drops on curve I and the corresponding drops on curves II and III, it was found necessary to estimate sigmas for the interpolated drops. The sigmas obtained for the actually measured drops on curve I, that is, for the drops between days 1-2, 2-3, 3-4, 4-5, 5-6, 6-7, were as follows: .237, .239, .247, .228, .190, and .187. It would seem, therefore, that to assume a sigma of .275 for an interpolated drop is more than fair.

Comparing, now, the drops in group II, days 7-8, and in group III, days 3-4, with the interpolated drops in group I corresponding to them, we have the results shown in table 4.

The critical ratio of 1.497, when interpreted in terms of probability, means that, if there were no real difference between the drop shown in group II, days 7-8, and that interpolated on the same level in group I, a difference as large as that shown in the table would occur by chance 671 times out of 10,000. This again suggests rather strongly that the drop between days 7-8 in group II is really greater than any corresponding drop in group I. It suggests, in short, that the drop between days 7-8 was evidence of a real *latent* learning which had already developed and was here being brought to light by the introduction of the reward.

TABLE 4

Mean errors

	Drop in errors	Drop	Difference between drop and that of Group I	Differ- ence	**Critical ratio**
Group II—days 7-8	1.416	.232	...	...	...
Group I—interpolated	.877	.275	.539	.360	**1.497**
Group III—days 3-4	1.520	.263	...	...	...
Group I—interpolated	.740	.275	.780	.381	**2.047**

Similarly, the critical ratio, 2.047, when interpreted in terms of probability, means that, if there were no real difference between the drop shown by group III, days 3-4, and that interpolated at the same level of the curve for group I, a difference as large as that shown in the table would occur by chance only 173 times out 10,000. This is a very strong indication that the drop between days 3-4 was evidence of a true latent learning having occurred in group III which was brought to light by the introduction of the reward.

Maze B: Groups I and II

To make sure that the differences just discussed were not due to any differences between the two groups arising from sampling, one of our experimental groups and the control group were tested in a second maze.

Thus, 22 rats of group II and 23 rats from group I were, subsequent to their practice in maze A, run in maze B. Both groups were run once a day and given food for two minutes in the food box at the end of each run. The learning curves are shown in figure 7, and are practically

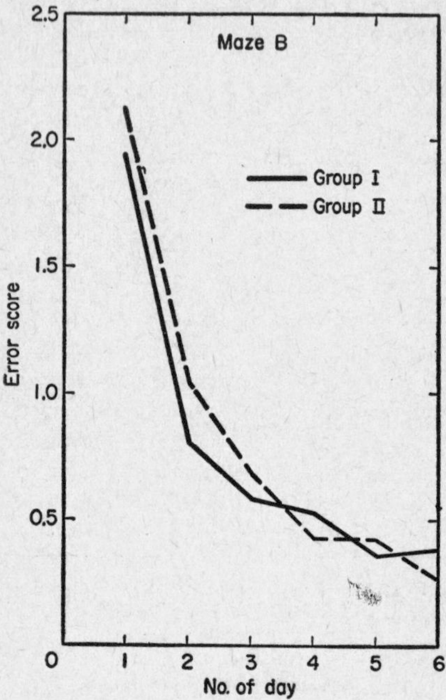

Fig. 7.

identical. We conclude that the differences in the groups in maze A were due to the *experimental conditions* and not to native differences between the groups.

Maze A: *Group IV*

Granted that the results so far discussed indicate that groups II and III acquired a latent learning during their non-reward periods which was made manifest when reward was introduced, questions still remain as to the nature of this latent learning. Was it the acquisition of mere general familiarity with the maze? Or was it the acquisition of a something more specific? To throw some light on these questions a fourth group of rats was run in maze A, viz., group IV.

Group IV consisted of 10 rats. Like group II, they were run for seven days without reward and then reward was introduced. But instead of being run during the non-reward period in the forward direction, they were, during this period, run in a *reverse direction.* That is, they were started at the food box (in this case empty, of course) and run to the starting box, where they received no reward. On the eighth day, their direction was changed to the *normal one* and they were given reward in the food box, as with group I. The hypothesis was that, if, upon being reversed to the normal direction and given reward, they then did decidedly better than the control group, it would suggest that the latent learning which showed itself in groups II and III upon reward may have been no more than a mere general familiarity which might have been acquired just as well through running the maze in the backward direction. If, on the contrary, they did *not* do decidedly better than the control, group I, when being run in the normal fashion, this would suggest that the latent learning developed by groups II and III was in part at least something more specific; something which could be developed by only the forward-going practice.

Table 5 gives the results of comparing errors for group

TABLE 5

Mean errors

Day	Group I	Day	Group IV	Difference	σ Difference	Critical ratio
1	2.97	8	2.80	.17	.46	.37
2	2.56	9	1.80	.76	.46	1.65
3	1.58	10	1.40	.18	.27	.68
4	1.03	11	1.10	.07	.38	.19
5	1.08	12	1.10	.02	.28	.06
6	.69	13	.50	.19	.27	.70
7	.30	14	.30	.005	.17	.03

IV (when running in the forward direction) with those for group I. Figure 8 gives the corresponding curves for group IV and group I, and for group II (after reward had been introduced).

It would appear that day 2 is the only one on which there is any significant superiority of group IV over group I. On that day the critical ratio of the difference in favor of group IV is 1.647. This, interpreted in terms of probability, means that, if there were no real difference between the groups, a difference as great as the one

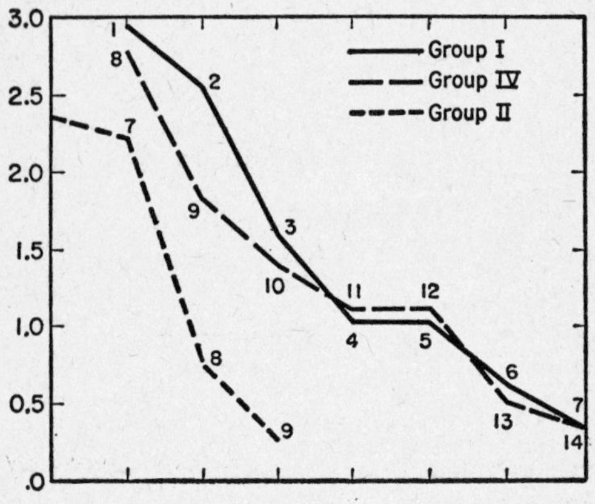

Fig. 8.

obtained would occur by chance 498 times out of 10,000.

One is therefore led to conclude that the increased familiarity with the maze gained by group IV in running backward probably did help to a *slight* extent on the second day of forward running. That is, group IV were somewhat better able than group I (probably because less distracted) to make use of their first day's experience in the forward direction. This superiority, however, did not persist. The initial advantage of familiarity possessed by group IV had disappeared on the third day, when their record was no better than that of group I.

Compare, now, in figure 8,[1] group IV with group II after the latter were rewarded. Group IV ran the maze for seven days without the "expectation" of reward in the forward direction. Comparing day 8 of group IV with day 7 of group II, it seems evident that the non-reward forward-running is the more helpful.[2] Six days of it is more valuable than seven days of backward-running. Further, not only does the non-reward forward-running give group II a decided head-start over group IV (which had had only backward non-reward running), but it also seems to cause them to continue to learn faster. In only two days group II accomplished an error elimination which it took group IV six days to achieve. Evidently the latent learning which group II developed as a result of their non-reward forward-running was decidedly more than the *general familiarity* which group IV seems to have acquired from their non-reward backward-running.

CONCLUSIONS

1. Non-reward running definitely develops a *latent learning*, and such latent learning is made manifest when reward is introduced.
2. Furthermore, it is evident that this latent learning is something more than a general familiarity such as might be acquired by backward-running through the maze.

The Two-Way Maze

A further question now arises. Given this latent learning, what are the laws of its acquisition? There is a well-known doctrine of animal trial-and-error learning,

[1] A comparison in terms of sigmas of the differences and critical ratios of the differences indicated in the figure was not presented in the table because at the time this final report was written, the original data for making such a comparison were no longer available.

[2] Although, as just mentioned, we have not the critical ratio for the difference.

viz., that the selection of the right path is either wholly[3] or in large part[4] dependent upon a greater frequency or recency of exercise upon the correct path than upon any one of the incorrect paths. Watson has also attempted to show that the situation in the ordinary maze is such as, by chance, to cause the animals to have greater frequencies and recencies upon the segments of the true paths than upon the blinds.

It seemed worth while, therefore, to try a different type of maze—a maze, that is, which could not, by the most strained interpretation, be supposed to give, as a result of *chance*, any greater exercise on the correct path than on the incorrect path. Such a maze is maze C (see Fig. 4).[5] We now turn to the conditions and results for maze C.

Maze C: Groups V *and* VI

Two groups of rats were run on maze C as follows:

Group V. *Control.*—This group consisted of 23 rats. They were run once a day for sixteen days. They were allowed to eat for *two minutes in the food box* and were then removed to another cage (not their living-cages) and allowed to finish their day's ration, after which they were returned to their living-cages.

Group VI. *Experimental.*—This group consisted of 21 rats (litter mates of those in group V). For the first sixteen days, they found no food in the food box but were kept in it without reward for two minutes. They were then removed to another cage (not the living-cage) where they were fed after an interval of approximately one hour. Only then were they finally returned to their living-cages. At the end of the sixteenth day's run

[3] This is, or was, Watson's (1914) contention.

[4] This is one way in which Thorndike's (1911) familiar law of exercise is frequently interpreted.

[5] This fact, that mazes such as C, which present alternative correct paths (one better than the other) rather than a correct path and blinds, do not, through the laws of chance, offer any greater frequency of exercise upon the finally chosen path than upon the finally discarded path, has been previously pointed out by Kuo (1922) and by Sams and Tolman (1925).

and on the runs on the four successive days, food was given in the food box in the same manner as with group V.

For about half the animals in each group, food box 1 on the left (see fig. 4) was used. And for the other half, food box 2 on the right was used. This was to eliminate so far as possible the effects of odor and tracking.

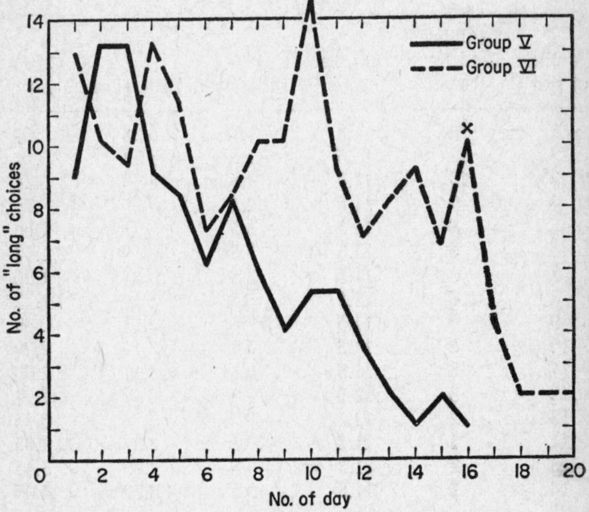

Fig. 9.

Scoring.—When a rat had passed the bifurcation into either the shorter or the longer alley, the trapdoor was closed and he was scored as having chosen either "long" or "short." His time from the starting box to the food was measured by a stop watch.

The results, in terms of numbers of "long" choices made by the group as a whole, are shown in tables 6 and 7 and in figure 9. These indicate a gradual improvement for the control group but very little improvement in the experimental group until reward was given, and then a very sudden improvement. That is, the general character of the results obtained with maze A were substantiated.

Furthermore, as table 7 shows, there was very little greater choosing of the short path by the experimental group until after the reward was introduced. In other words, the latent propensity of group VI to take the shorter route, which was made manifest as soon as reward was introduced, was developed in the course of exercise which only slightly (if at all) favored this shorter route. It seems evident that the practice which developed latent learning did not achieve this latent learning by means of the action of selective frequency.

TABLE 6

Improvement of scores by Group V

Number of run	Number of "long" choices	Chance score	Difference	Difference	Critical ratio
1	10	11.5	1.5	3.38	.44
2	13	11.5	1.5	3.38	.44
3	13	11.5	1.5	3.38	.44
4	9	11.5	2.5	3.35	.75
5	8	11.5	3.5	3.31	1.06
6	6	11.5	5.5	3.19	1.72
7	8	11.5	3.5	3.31	1.06
8	6	11.5	5.5	3.19	1.72
9	4	11.5	7.5	3.01	2.49
10	5	11.5	6.5	3.11	2.09
11	5	11.5	6.5	3.11	2.09
12	3	11.5	8.5	2.89	2.94
13	2	11.5	9.5	2.75	3.45
14	1	11.5	10.5	2.59	4.05
15	2	11.5	9.5	2.75	3.45
16	1	11.5	10.5	2.59	4.05

SUMMARY

1. Rats run under a non-reward condition learned much more slowly than rats run under a reward condition. This held for both errors and time.

TABLE 7

Improvement of scores by Group VI

Number of run	Number of "long" choices	Chance score	Difference	Difference	Critical ratio
1	13	10.5	+2.5	3.20	.78
2	10	10.5	−.5	3.24	.15
3	9	10.5	−1.5	3.22	.46
4	13	10.5	+2.5	3.20	.78
5	11	10.5	+.5	3.24	.15
6	7	10.5	−3.5	3.15	1.11
7	8	10.5	−2.5	3.20	.78
8	10	10.5	−.5	3.24	.15
9	10	10.5	−.5	3.24	.15
10	14	10.5	+3.5	3.15	1.11
11	9	10.5	−1.5	3.22	.46
12	7	10.5	−3.5	3.15	1.11
13	9	10.5	−1.5	3.22	.46
14	10	10.5	+.5	3.24	.15
15	7	10.5	−3.5	3.15	1.11
16	11	10.5	+.5	3.24	.15
17	4	10.5	+6.5	2.90	2.24
18	2	10.5	+8.5	2.66	3.20
19	2	10.5	+8.5	2.66	3.20
20	2	10.5	+8.5	2.66	3.20

2. Rats previously run under a non-reward condition, when suddenly rewarded made a great improvement. On the first day after the introduction of the reward their drop in mean error was greater than that made by the control group on any single day.

3. This fact seems to indicate that, during the non-reward period, the rats were developing a *latent* learning of the maze which they were able to utilize as soon as reward was introduced.

4. This latent learning, however, was something more than a general familiarity with the maze such as might be acquired by running through it in a backward direction. For a group of rats run through backward under non-reward conditions did not show any such improvement when run through in the forward direction and rewarded.

5. It was demonstrated by the use of the two-path maze that the latent learning which was developed under non-reward conditions and was made manifest as soon as reward was introduced was not the result of any very consistently greater frequency of the correct over the incorrect path during the non-reward period. It resulted, that is, from a non-reward practice which favored almost equally, both the "incorrect" and the "correct" path.

LITERATURE CITED

Kuo, Z. Y.
1922 "The Nature of Unsuccessful Acts and their Order of Elimination in Animal Learning." *Jour. Comp. Psychol.*, 2: 1-27.

Lashley, K. S.
1918 "A Simple Maze: with Data on the Relation of the Distribution of Practice to the Rate of Learning." *Psychobiology*, 1: 353-367.

Peterson, Joseph
1918 "Effect of Length of Blind Alleys on Maze Learning." *Behav. Monogr.*, 3: 1-53.

Sams, C. F., and Tolman, E. C.
1925 "Time Discrimination in White Rats." *Jour. Comp. Psychol.*, 5: 225-264.

Simmons, R.
1924 "The Relative Effectiveness of Certain Incentives in Animal Learning." *Comp. Psychol. Mon.*, 2: 1-79.

Szymanski, J. S.
1918 "Versuche über die Wirkung der Faktoren, die als Antrich zum Erlernen einer Handlung dienen konnen." Pflüger's *Archiv f. d. gesamte Physiologie*, 171: 374-385.

Thorndike, E. L.
1911 *Animal Intelligence*, p. 244.

Watson, J. B.
1914 *Behavior*, chap. vii.

6

Studies in Learning and Motivation: I. Equal Reinforcements in Both Endboxes, Followed by Shock in One Endbox

EDWARD C. TOLMAN AND HENRY GLEITMAN
University of California

INTRODUCTION

A number of studies have been published during the last several years designed to test certain aspects of the sign-Gestalt theory of learning—in particular the phenomenon of 'latent learning.' [1] Based for the most part on an experimental test proposed some time ago by White (16), these recent studies have used a rather simple experimental situation. A rat is placed in a one-choice T-maze or Y-maze containing food at one end and water at the other. If the animal is run thirsty until he has learned to turn towards the side containing water—adequate measures being taken to insure objectively equal experience with both sides—, what will be his response later when he is satiated for water but deprived of *food* and again run in the maze? The experimental answer to this question was first provided by Spence and Lippitt (10), who found that, in correspondence with the

This article originally appeared in The *Journal* of Experimental Psychology, 39, 1949, pp. 810-819.

[1] The concept of latent learning was originated by Blodgett (1) and he presented the first experimental evidence for it. His findings were subsequently confirmed by others, for example, Tolman and Honzik (12). And the senior author (11) relied upon these early findings *re* latent learning as basic support for his sign-Gestalt, or expectancy, theory of learning.

predictions of Hull's (3) reinforcement theory, all their animals continued to run to the side on which they had been originally rewarded.[2] These authors interpreted their results as indicating that the animals had not learned the location of the food during their original training period. For the most part this conclusion seems to have been confirmed by later investigators. Walker (14) and Kendler (4) obtained similar results using somewhat different maze set-ups from one another and from the original Spence and Lippitt maze, and Kendler and Mencher (5) showed that such results could not be ascribed to a mere lack of perceptual acquaintance with the food as Leeper (6) had suggested. On the whole, then, it seems probable that rats do not readily learn the location of one type of goal-object when under another different drive. We must conclude that at least in such situations it is relatively difficult to obtain evidence of latent learning.[3]

The failure of such experimental situations to demonstrate latent learning has been considered by some writers as an argument against the possibility of latent learning under any conditions and therefore as a severe blow to the sign-Gestalt theory of learning. However, while it is true that a prediction made by sign-Gestalt theorists

[2] It is to be emphasized that these results actually correspond with Hull's theory only if it be assumed that the specific S_D for thirst did not become an important item in the original habit formed. Otherwise, the change from the thirst S_D to the hunger S_D should have caused some breakdown in the tendency to take the water side. Spence and Lippitt get around this by speaking of a 'generalized drive' resulting from thirst and being the same when the hunger was subsequently introduced.

[3] A further experiment by Walker (15), as yet unpublished, reported at the A.P.A. meetings, September 1948, did, however, demonstrate latent learning in a similar set-up. Hungry rats did learn the location of food when run thirsty to water, so that when later made hungry they chose the food side. In his set-up there were no forced trials. Water was on both sides. But in getting to the water in the preliminary training they went through a food compartment on one side and did not on the other. And then when made hungry they chose the side where the food compartment was. (Private communication from Walker.)

has been tested and found erroneous, this does not necessarily invalidate the basic concepts underlying the theory. For the sign-Gestalt theory does not necessitate the assertion that latent learning will occur in every instance, but insists merely that reinforcement is not a necessary condition of *all* learning. On the other hand, the reinforcement theorist is forced by the very nature of his doctrine to deny the possibility of latent learning in any instance whatever.

It was the purpose of the present investigation to find an experimental situation relatively similar to the Spence and Lippitt set-up that would demonstrate latent learning, and to attempt to determine some of the factors which might contribute to its presence or absence in such situations.

Let us consider the different interpretations suggested for a rat's mastery of a T-maze. According to the reinforcement theory what is learned is a sequence of responses leading to reinforcement. In terms of the choice situation, what is learned is the correct turning response as opposed to the wrong one. The correct one leads to a reinforcing state of affairs, the wrong one does not, and accordingly the stimulus complex presented at the choice point acquires a greater tendency to evoke the reinforced turn. Presumably no differentiation between the responses could be obtained if either response were equally rewarded or reward withheld from both—nothing should be learned in such a situation. On the other hand, the sign-Gestalt theory holds that the rat learns not only the correct turn, but also other perceptual relationships within the maze, regardless of their reward value; he forms what the senior author has recently called a 'cognitive map' (13). In other words, the animal acts as if he has some 'notion' as to what each side contains —this 'notion' being demonstrated (either during the training situation as in the orthodox maze learning curve or in later performance as in the latent learning experiments) by the appropriate turn at the choice point. It is clear that our knowledge is as yet inadequate to predict the precise nature of rats' 'notions'—i.e., which perceptual differences will be learned in this manner, under what motivational states, and the like. However, the sign-Gestalt theory can at least make the very general statement that *some* perceptual relationships will tend to be learned.

Perhaps one can then restate the latent learning hypothesis in its most general form: Under *certain* conditions, *some* discriminanda or the *relationships between some discriminanda* will be learned by the organism even though these discriminanda bear no differential relationship to reinforcement. This is admittedly a very general and a very cautious statement of the hypothesis. However, it is considered fruitful in so much as it offers a framework for further investigation of the particular conditions surrounding its application. And despite this statement's generality, reinforcement theory would nonetheless be forced to deny it.

PURPOSE AND GENERAL PLAN OF EXPERIMENT

I. The primary purpose of the present experiment was to find a situation within which the discriminanda differences are such as to be learned by rats, even though these differences are not related to reinforcement.

The plan of experiment was modelled somewhat after the Maier reasoning experiments (7), involving the integration of two experiences:

A. Situation 1: The animals were run in a maze containing two highly differentiated end-boxes. This differentiation, however, was not related to reinforcement.

B. Situation 2: Subsequent to Situation 1, the animals were placed in one of the end-boxes and were given an electric shock, while finding food in the other end-box. This Situation was presented in another room.

C. Test situation: Subsequent to Situation 2, the animals were again placed into the maze, and their choice rewarded.

II. An additional attempt was made to determine whether differences in strength of motivation in the original learning would have any bearing on the later avoidance in the test situation of the side leading to the end-box in which the animals had experienced the shock.[4]

[4] An as yet unpublished experiment of this same design was earlier carried out in the California laboratory by R. J. Schweers.

APPARATUS

The design of the apparatus to be used for this experiment posed a certain problem. It was necessary to design a maze the end-boxes of which were as perceptually differentiated as possible, yet to be sure at the same time that these differences were not perceptible from the choice point. Failure to control this latter factor adequately would render any results inconclusive, inasmuch as positive results might then be due either to true latent learning under Situation 1, or merely to the recent experience under Situation 2. The latter results could easily be explained on a reinforcement basis—as a response away from a stimulus at the choice point that had been contiguous with punishment in Situation 2. On the other hand, if a difference be not apparent from the choice point, then a positive reaction (i.e., the animal running away from the side containing the end-box he was shocked in) can only be attributed to learning under Situation 1, a possibility denied by reinforcement theory.[5]

The results he obtained were similar to those we shall report. Schweers, therefore, deserves credit for suggesting our experiment.

An abstract of an experiment of a somewhat similar nature by Seward (9) has also appeared. His animals were first allowed to explore a T-maze having two different end-boxes and then rewarded in one of them. The animals were then started from the entrance to the maze and a large majority then ran to the side on which they had been fed. In short, he also obtained latent learning.

[5] It is to be pointed out that the design of our experiment is closely related to that of an earlier experiment by Honzik and Tolman (2). In the Honzik and Tolman experiment hungry rats also ran a T-maze obtaining food at either end of the arms of the T. In this experiment, however, one of the arms of the T was shorter than the other, so that the animals developed a strongly preferred side. The animals were then shocked in the end-box on this preferred side—with this end-box,(however, *in situ* and not as in the present experiment in another room. When then started again on the leg of the T a large proportion of the animals ran to the other, or non-shocked, side. However, it appeared from a series of control experiments also carried out that these results were dependent

The apparatus used consisted of a simple alley maze, as shown in Fig. 1. The two end-sections A and B contained the two end-boxes and a 22-in. runway to each.

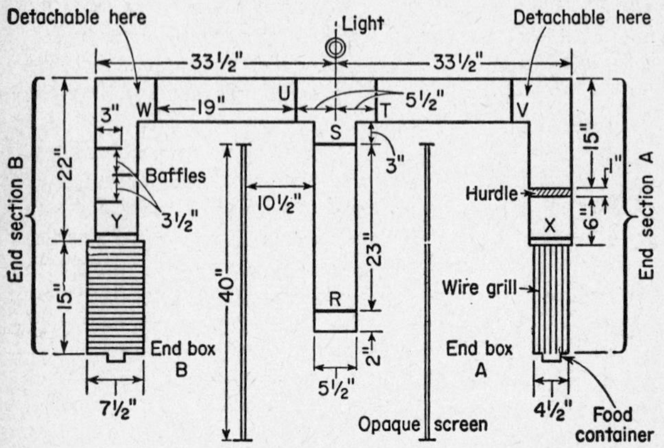

Fig. 1. Floorplan of maze

R, S, T, U, V, W, X and Y are one-way doors. Some other dimensions of the apparatus not indicated on the diagram are as follows:

The maze walls were 6 in. high. The hurdle in End-section A was 2½ in. high. The wires in each grill in the end-boxes were separated by ½ in., there being nine wires in End-box A, 20 in End-box B. All the one-way doors were hinged at a point 5½ in. from the floor, excepting only one-way door X, which was smaller and was hinged at a point 3½ in. from the floor.

Both of the end-sections could be detached from the maze in their entirety. A small box was set into the far wall of each of the two end-boxes to serve as a food con-

---

upon general visual cues. And, since there was directional lighting in the room, it appears to the present writers that such results may well have been due to some common features between the visual cues at the end-box where the animals were shocked and those on the path which led to this end-box. Hence the present prescriptions were not fully fulfilled by the Honzik and Tolman experiment.

tainer. The floor of both end-boxes was fitted with a wire grill, to allow shocking the animals during the second part of the experiment.

One-way doors made of aluminum were hinged at points R, S, T, U, V, W, X, and Y to prevent retracing. Doors T and U could be locked by the experimenter when necessary to permit forced trials to the opposite side. Doors X and Y were painted black, all others were white.

An effort was made to create the greatest possible perceptual differences between the two end-sections. End-section A was painted black and was totally unilluminated except for whatever stray light might enter through the small food container opening. The end-box in section A was narrower than that in section B and the grill was fitted in parallel lines to the end-runway. Furthermore, a little hurdle, about 2½ in. high and ½ in. thick, was placed in the middle of the runway, and the one-way door X, leading from the end-runway to the end-box, was smaller and hinged lower than the corresponding one for end-box B.

In contrast end-section B was left unpainted, and the end-box of the section was strongly illuminated by a 60 watt bulb set into a housing on the cover of the end-box. The wire grill in end-box B was fitted perpendicularly to the runway. In addition three baffles were placed in the end-runway of that section, which forced a sort of snaky movement from the animals in contrast to the jumping movement necessitated by the hurdle in section A. The one-way door Y, leading from the runway to end-box B, was larger than the corresponding one in Section A and had a velvet black curtain attached to it on the inside.

The black curtain and the baffles, furthering on the one hand the perceptual differentiation of the two end-sections, also served the additional purpose of preventing light from the illuminated goal-box reaching the choice point area. To separate further the end-box cues from those provided at the choice point, two opaque screens 26 by 38 in. were set up between the initial runway and the end-sections, as shown in Fig. 1. Both end-sections were covered with black cloth. The only source of general illumination in the room came from a 150-watt bulb, mounted in a reflector directly behind the choice point, and facing upwards.

To test for any possible illumination differences at the choice point, photographs were taken of the choice point area under the actual illumination conditions of the experiment. Two strips of white paper were placed in the center of the choice point, facing 45 degrees to each side, and were photographed to indicate the difference in illumination at each side of the choice point. The photographs were later covered up with tape so that only the two strips were visible, and presented to judges who were asked to indicate which of the two sides was brighter. Judgments of 'equal' were permitted. Of 15 judges, most of whom were psychology graduate students, but who were totally ignorant of the purpose of their judgments, 3 judged *A* brighter than *B*, 3 judged *B* brighter than A, and the remaining 9 judged them equal.

A test of possible temperature differences at the choice point was also made by the insertion of thermometers. No differences were found.

ANIMALS

A total of 31 experimentally naive, male virgin rats from the U.C. laboratory, ranging in age from four to six months of M by M Tryon stock, were used for this experiment. All animals were placed on a 24-hour food deprivation schedule for several days prior to the onset of the experiment, and were fed daily about three a.m. on the regular dry food fed the colony.

PROCEDURE

A. *Preliminary Training*

Prior to the actual experiment the animals were trained on a 28-in. straight alley, containing two white one-way doors, and leading to a goal box with a food container set into the far wall. The end-box used was essentially similar to those used in the maze proper, except that it was of intermediate width, 6 by 15 in., and contained no wire grill. The cover of the end-box was made of mesh wire, and the rats were run under ordinary conditions of room illumination—six overhead lamps providing the illumination of the room and the end-boxes for this phase of the experiment. The rats were all run under 24 hours of hunger. Each animal was run about four times nightly, for seven nights.

The food given to the animals in the end-boxes was in the form of small pellets, consisting of a mixture of their regular dry food, and some lactose added as a binding agent. Each of the pellets weighed 135 milligrams, and contained 10 parts ordinary dry food to 4 parts of lactose. During this preliminary training situation the animals were permitted to consume as many pellets as they chose.

B. Procedure of Experiment Proper

Situation 1.—The animals were divided into two groups, run under 48 and 12 hours food deprivation respectively, on alternate mornings between 12:30 and 6 A.M. Each animal received two trials per experimental day, one free and one forced for nine experimental days. In the free trial, which was presented first each day, the animal chose whichever side it wanted. On the subsequent forced trial, the door (T or U) leading to the side chosen on the preceding free trial was locked.

Food was placed in both end-boxes. To insure equal food reinforcement on both sides, equal amounts of food were presented at all times—two pellets per trial for each animal.

The animals were given an upper limit of one hour to pass through the maze. If an animal failed to do so twice in succession, it was discarded from the experiment. In this manner 6 rats were lost, 4 from the 12 hour hunger group, and 2 from the 48 hour animals. The data presented are for the 25 rats remaining—13 rats in Group I (48 hours of hunger) and 12 in Group II (12 hours of hunger).

Situation 2.—About 26 hours following the completion of their ninth day's trials, all of the animals in each group were subjected to Situation 2—being shocked in one of the end-boxes. For this phase of the experiment, all animals were under a 24-hour hunger drive.

For this purpose, the entire end-sections A and B were

removed from the maze and placed on *separate tables in another room.* The two tables were about five feet apart and arranged *at right angles to each other.* The sole illumination of the room was provided by the same lighting arrangement as was used in Situation 1, the light being mounted equidistant from each of the end-sections.

Each animal was first placed at the entrance of one of the end-sections, and received food when he reached the end-box. After a one-min. interval, he was then placed at the entrance of the other end-section, and received a violent electric shock about five sec. after he entered its end-box. He was detained in this end-box for one min., being shocked at intervals for a total of 20 sec. After about five min. he was placed in the same end-box again by hand, and was again shocked for 20 sec. out of a total 60 sec. of further detention there.

Half of the animals were shocked in end-box A and the other in end-box B. To equate for possible effects of position preferences, the free choices during the nine days of running in Situation 1 were tabulated. An index of side preference was then assigned to each animal on the basis of the total number of free runs to end-box B during those nine days. The animals in each of the two hunger-deprivation groups (12 hours and 48 hours) were then split into two sub-groups, one sub-group being shocked in end-box A and the other in end-box B, in such a manner that the average position preference was approximately the same for the two sub-groups within each main group.

Test situation.—Approximately two hours after completion of Situation 2, the animals were run again on the maze, set up exactly as in Situation 1, in the same room in which Situation 1 was conducted, and with the end-sections fitted back into place. All animals in both groups had been deprived of food for 26 hours, except for 2 pellets of food which had been consumed in the harmless end-box in Situation 2.

RESULTS

In the test situation the great majority (22 out of 25) of the animals turned to the side opposite to that which contained the end-box they had been shocked in. Only three animals entered the wrong side at the choice point. One of these, an animal from Group I (48 hours of deprivation in the original learning situation), after having entered the wrong door at the choice point, squealed and started to bite and scratch at the door which it had just passed through, furiously trying to open it, managing eventually to squeeze through a slight clearing between the top of the door and the maze cover, and then dashed over to the correct side.

No particular difference was found in the test situation between Group I (48 hours of food deprivation in Situation 1) and Group II (12 hours of deprivation in Situation 1). Eleven out of 13 animals in Group I, and 11 out of 12 animals in Group II, made the correct turn at the choice point. Accordingly it was thought justifiable to combine the results of both groups for a test of significance. The probability of non-chance selection of the harmless side is indicated by a chi-square of 14.47, which is highly significant for one degree of freedom.

No particular distinguishing feature was noted for the three rats that ran to the wrong side. Neither their position preference, nor their time of running during the original training situation, yields any basis of differentiation from the rest of the animals.

DISCUSSION

The results seem to indicate that the primary purpose of the experiment had been achieved. A situation was found, within which the discriminanda differences and relations are such as to be learned by rats, even though these differences are not differentially related to reinforcement. While it is true that the animals were rewarded in the maze, they were rewarded equally on both sides, so that neither the right nor the left turn was reinforced differentially. The fact that one end-box was lit up, contained baffles, etc., had no bearing on the reward received.

Of course it might be argued that the discriminanda differences of and by themselves constituted a reinforcement. A case for this is easily made, since at least some animals seemed to acquire position preferences for the one or the other side. Reinforcement theory would hold then that a particular turn became reinforced at the choice point, due to the animals' dislike of strong light, or of baffles, etc.

Nevertheless, this assumption does not explain the behavior of the animals during the test situation. For, even if the choice responses were differentially reinforced, we should only expect a continuation of the acquired preference, rather than the obtained shift to the harmless side. Furthermore, only about half of the animals showed any particular side preference, but even those animals that seemed to be indifferent to the sides, during the original training situation (Situation 1), made the correct choice during the test situation.

Of further interest is the fact that, due to the particular arrangement of the baffles in end-section B, the last turning responses of the animals just before entering the end-box must be a right turn. The first trial in Situation 2 involved placing the animal at the beginning of the end-section, so that this turn had to be made just before entering the box and being shocked. By reinforcement theory, one might expect that this response, being followed by shock, would tend to be avoided. However, in the test situation, this response is precisely the one utilized by those animals that were shocked in end-box B. End-section B being located on the left of the choice point, a right turn was required to run towards the other side. In short, the animals acted as if they had remembered that the bright, baffle-containing box was on the left, and the dark, hurdle-containing box on the right. It is obviously impossible to state which of the various available discriminanda differences were remembered by the animals. Nor is it our purpose now to determine in detail precisely what cues were responded to and noticed —the main point is that enough stimulus differences were provided so that the animals could notice something. Thus, it seems that the very general statement of the latent learning hypothesis presented above has been verified. And despite the extreme generality of this statement, it seems to us relatively difficult to envisage an interpretation derived from the reinforcement theory from which these same results could have been equally easily predicted.

It must be admitted, however, that as yet no specific predictions can be made concerning the nature of the factors under which latent learning will appear, and those under which it will not. Eventually, sign-Gestalt theory will have the responsibility of providing more specific sub-hypotheses which will predict such outcomes. Thus, the results of the present experiment, in establishing the occurrence of latent learning in one situation, point to the need of a program of systematic research to discover the essential factors that will facilitate or inhibit its occurrence in any situation.

While certain speculations can be made concerning the nature of these relevant variables, such speculations are as yet more in the nature of hunches than of adequate theoretical formulations. We would suspect, for example, that the degree of motivation of the animal, the presence of an appropriate goal-object when he is to learn the location of an inappropriate one, the perceptual outstandingness of the object to be learned and the ability of the rat to discriminate or not to discriminate his drives are all factors of importance in determining whether or not latent learning will occur. And the present experiment did in fact seek to test one of these more specific possibilities—namely that different degrees of motivation will in some degree determine whether or not latent learning is obtained. However, our results showed no differences between the 12-hour and the 48-hour groups. We would believe, however, that these findings of ours do not necessarily rule out the possibility of motivation effects in other experiments. Perhaps the present problem was too simple and hence obscured whatever results from the motivation differences might have otherwise appeared. A further experiment is planned, utilizing an experimental situation that presents a greater problem to the animal—less markedly differentiated end-boxes and less experience in the maze.

Finally, all these considerations suggest a reinterpretation of the Spence and Lippitt and Kendler experiments. Intended to demonstrate the non-existence of latent learning, they seem rather to point to a program of further research to determine more specifically under what conditions latent learning will and will not occur. Such further research would lead perhaps to more specific sub-hypotheses concerning the nature and genesis of sign-Gestalten.

It is to be recalled that some years ago Miller (8) performed an experiment which had features similar to ours, the results of which he explained in reinforcement terms plus the assumption of anticipatory goal-responses. Miller ran animals in a straight-away either to a food device or to a water device. The final movements necessary to obtain food or water were quite different in the two end-devices. In the food device the animals had to climb up and make a sharp turn to the right to secure food. In the water device they went straight in and made a sharp turn to the left. In the main experiment half of the animals were shocked in the food device in a separate position and half in the water device. When put back on the initial straight-away those animals which had originally run the straight-away to food and had been then shocked in the food device now ran more slowly than those others which had also originally run to food and had been then shocked in the water device. And comparable results were obtained for the two sub-groups that had been trained to water one of which was shocked in the water device and the other in the food device.

Miller explains his results by assuming that a component of the given goal-response of turning right for food or turning left for water for which the animal had originally been trained on the alley became conditioned to the stimuli presented along the course of the alley. He also assumes that the internal proprioceptive stimuli resulting from such goal-responses become part of the stimuli to which the avoidance response (due to the shock) become conditioned. Then, when the animals are put back in the original straight-away, the stimuli from this straight-away evoke an anticipatory element of the final goal-response. This anticipatory element of the conditioned goal-response produces its own proprioceptive stimulus consequences. These now evoke, due to the experience of having been shocked in the box, a conditioned avoidance response which latter expresses itself in the animals' now running more slowly down the alley.

An especial feature of Miller's argument is that the two very distinctive goal-responses made by the animals in the two end-boxes produce two very distinctive anticipatory goal-responses with two very different resultant proprioceptive stimuli. One of these sets of proprioceptive stimuli gets conditioned in the shock situation to avoidance and the other does not.

Now it must be admitted that our own experiment involved a somewhat similar set-up. The approach to end-box A involved a hurdle and the approach to end-box B involved baffles. Hence, Miller could argue that our rats also had acquired two different anticipatory goal-responses —one conditioned to the stimuli at door T and the other conditioned to the stimuli at door U; and that in the shocking experience those animals which were shocked in end-box A got the proprioceptive stimuli resulting from the A goal-responses conditioned to avoidance whereas the others, who were shocked in end-box B, got the proprioceptive stimuli resulting from the B goal-response conditioned to avoidance. Then when put back in the maze and coming to the choice point and releasing their anticipatory goal-responses the A-shocked group had avoidance evoked when they faced the stimuli of the right hand path and the B-shocked group had avoidance evoked when they faced the stimuli of the left hand path. We cannot altogether deny the possibility of such an explanation. Absolutely to settle the issue it would be necessary to repeat our experiment where the two end-boxes differed in 'perceptual' characters only and where absolutely no differences of goal response in the two boxes would be involved. However, it may be noted that in Seward's experiment (see above, footnote 4) it was found that white and black goal boxes when the rats were fed in one and not in the other gave as positive latent learning results as did a pair of goal boxes which did produce different types of overt responses.

However, it may be asked what about blinking, pupillary reactions or the like? Is it possible to have a perceptual 'awareness' of any sort without concomitant motor responses? If it is Miller's (or Seward's) argument that there are such differentiating motor accompaniments for all perceptual processes, then these authors can perhaps hold, if they want to, that what we have called sign-Gestalten are based upon chains of minimal anticipatory responses going on at a very covert level. We, personally, are interested in the functional significance of latent learning and the resultant functional concept of sign-Gestalten and not in extremely hypothetical notions concerning the underlying neurology.

SUMMARY

1. Twenty-five hungry pigmented M by M Tryon stock rats were run in a covered T maze to equal food reinforcements at the two ends of the T. The two end-sections were strongly differentiated. The end-boxes were of different size and one had a bright light shining into it and the other was dark. The two entrance sections to these end-boxes also differed. One had baffles and the other a hurdle, and the doors into the end-boxes were somewhat different in size and manner of being hinged.

2. After equal training on the two sides—one free trial and one forced trial per day for nine days—the two end-sections were placed in another room. Half of the rats were shocked in one of the end-boxes and half in the other.

3. When placed back on the maze 22 out of a total of 25 rats immediately avoided the side leading to the box in which they had just been shocked. In this test trial all animals were run under equal drive strength—i.e., 26 hours of food deprivation.

4. In the original training the total group had been divided into two motivation groups—one 48 hours hungry when originally trained in the maze and the other 12 hours hungry. No differences in the later avoidance of the side leading to the box in which the animals had been shocked appeared between the two motivation groups.

5. Our general theoretical position is that, although the Spence and Lippitt (10), Kendler (4), Kendler and Mencher (5) and Walker (14) experiments have indi-

cated that 'latent learning' under the conditions of their experiments did not appear, this does not disprove the possibility of latent learning appearing under other conditions. All that the sign-Gestalt (or field expectancy) theory of learning assumes is that under some conditions, latent learning—that is learning which does not involve the differential reinforcement of responses—can nevertheless take place.

6. The present experiment seems to have provided such a set of conditions.

7. It is suggested that many further experiments varying such factors as the type of maze set-up, the amounts of initial training, degrees of motivation, forced or non-forced trials, the presence or absence of a reward object for the drive under which the animals are initially trained, and the like are needed in order to discover the precise conditions under which a non-differentially rewarded picking up of discriminanda and discriminanda relationships (i.e., latent learning) will or will not tend to appear.

REFERENCES

1. BLODGETT, H. C. The effect of the introduction of reward upon the maze performance of rats. *Univ. Calif. Publ. Psychol.*, 1929, 4, 113-134.
2. HONZIK, C. H., & TOLMAN, E. C. The perception of spatial relations by the rat: a type of response not easily explained by conditioning. *J. comp. Psychol.*, 1936, 22, 287-318.
3. HULL, C. L. Principles of behavior. New York: D. Appleton-Century Company, 1943.
4. KENDLER, H. H. An investigation of latent learning in a T-maze. *J. comp. physiol. Psychol.*, 1947, 40, 265-270.
5. KENDLER, H. H., & MENCHER, H. C. The ability of rats to learn the location of food when motivated by thirst. An experimental reply to Leeper. *J. exp. Psychol.*, 1948, 38, 82-88.
6. LEEPER, R. W. The experiments by Spence and Lippitt and by Kendler on the sign-Gestalt theory of learning. *J. exp. Psychol.*, 1948, 38, 102-105.

7. MAIER, N. R. F. Reasoning and learning. *Psychol. Rev.*, 1931, 38, 332-346.
8. MILLER, N. E. A reply to "Sign-Gestalt or conditioned reflex?" *Psychol. Rev.*, 1935, 42, 280-292.
9. SEWARD, J. P. The minimum requirement for learning a maze discrimination. *Amer. Psychologist*, 1947, 2, 409.
10. SPENCE, K. W., & LIPPITT, R. O. An experimental test of the sign-gestalt theory of trial and error learning. *J. exp. Psychol.*, 1946, 36, 491-502.
11. TOLMAN, E. C. *Purposive behavior in animals and men.* New York: The Century Co., 1932.
12. TOLMAN, E. C., & HONZIK, C. H. Introduction and removal of reward and maze performance in rats. *Univ. Calif. Publ. Psychol.*, 1930, 4, 257-275.
13. TOLMAN, E. C. Cognitive maps in rats and men. *Psychol. Rev.*, 1948, 55, 189-208.
14. WALKER, E. L. Drive specificity and learning. *J. exp. Psychol.*, 1948, 38, 39-49.
15. WALKER, E. L. The acquisition of a response to food under conditions of food satiation. *Amer. Psychologist*, 1948, 3, 239. (Reported by title only)
16. WHITE, R. K. The case for the Tolman-Lewin interpretation of learning. *Psychol. Rev.*, 1943, 50, 157-186.

7

On the Elimination of Cul Entries without Obvious Reinforcement[1]

KENNETH MACCORQUODALE AND
PAUL E. MEEHL
University of Minnesota

In the course of a series of maze experiments we made an interesting incidental observation. Five naive, hungry rats had been permitted to explore freely a replica of the six-unit multiple T-maze used by Blodgett (1). There was no food or water present. After four uninterrupted hours of such exploration, the animals were removed from wherever they happened to be in the maze and placed in a large, unfamiliar cage which was not furnished with food or water. When the first rat was subsequently placed in the entry box of the maze, he made a rather rapid, errorless run to the goal, without any retracing. This behavior was sufficiently dramatic to lead us to "run" the other four, who made a total of eight errors out of a possible thirty, which is significantly better than chance ($p < .02$).

It was suggested to us that, for the albino rat, entrance into a blind alley, with its resulting hindrance of locomotion and occasional straining in turning around, may constitute a mild negative reinforcement; and that unimpeded forward movement may have a "self-rewarding" character based possibly upon such drives as *exploration* and *activity*. The three experiments here reported were conducted to establish the reality of the effect by exclud-

---

This article originally appeared in The *Journal* of Comparative Physiological Psychology, 44, 1951, pp. 367-371.

[1] This study was made possible through a research grant by the Graduate School of the University of Minnesota.

ing any "obvious" rewards but without attempting to determine just what reinforcements are operating.

EXPERIMENT I

Method

Five male albino rats, about 100 days old, experimentally naive, were used. After 28 hours of food deprivation (employed merely to maintain a high level of activity), each rat was placed in a replica of the Blodgett maze, the doors being locked open throughout the experiment. An observer sat on a chair which was placed upon a table beside the maze, and the other experimenter left the room after placing the rat in the maze, at the third cul. The subject was allowed to explore freely for 30 min. on two successive days while experimenter kept a continuous record of all locomotion, differentiating three depths of blind-alley penetration. At the end of the 30 min. the rat was removed from the maze, care being taken not to remove him from a cul or when he was in either the stem to the goal or entry box. Upon removal he was placed in a small wooden box and carried to another room, where he remained for ½-hr.; he was then placed in an empty cage other than the home cage for 2 hr. before being returned to the home cage. After the lapse of 2½ additional hours on the second day, the rats were given a test trial by being placed singly in the entrance box and allowed to move about in the maze freely until they entered the goal box.

Results

Since retracing was possible and all five rats retraced at some point, it is desirable to analyze the data from the test trial in several ways. If we consider only those responses made at the first exposure to a given choice point, there are 30 choices (6 per rat for five rats) with a "chance" expectancy of 15 errors. Defining an "error" as a cul penetration to rat length excluding tail, only 6 errors were made (20 per cent of those possible), which is significantly better than chance ($p < .01$). If we include "second chance" (i.e., following retracing) forward-going errors, we find that the five rats had 48 such opportunities, of which 12 were errors (25 per cent of possible), which is also significantly better than chance ($p < .01$). Finally, if we consider all errors, both forward and backward, first and second choices, of 60 possible occasions of choice, 13 were errors (22 per cent of possible errors), which is significantly different from chance ($p < .01$).

Another way to approach these data is to compute the deviation from zero of the mean of the "gains" made by individual rats between the first exploratory day and the test run. The difference between number of cul entries on first exposure to any unit on the first day and that for first exposures during the test run is significant at the 2 per cent level ($t = 3.76$, *df*). However, counting, as above, first exposures on the free exploration day will include some approaches to units from the direction opposite from that of the test run; there is no reason to believe that the probabilities of entering a cul are the same if it is approached from two different directions. Therefore, we have compared the gains made in number of cul entries on first *forward-going* exposure to a unit for the first exploratory run versus the first exposure on the test run. The significance of this difference is between the 5 and 10 per cent levels, although the average "improvement" is 1.2 cul entries per rat.

The observers, during the two periods of free exploration, had a strong impression that as the time wore on, the rats spent increasingly less time in the culs and proportionately more in the "correct" path and in the end boxes. We have calculated for each rat a ratio whose numerator is the sum of the weights assigned to cul penetrations of differing depths for a constant interval of time, and whose denominator is an expression of actual distance travelled in that time. A drop in this ratio, from one observation period to a later one, should indicate roughly the rat's tendency to stay out of the culs while he is moving about in the maze. A *t*-test of the drops in this ratio between the first 5 min. of the first day and the test run was not significant, being between the 5 and 10 per cent levels, although each of the five rats reduced the size of its ratio.

Unfortunately, during the first free-exploration day these animals made more entries into the goal box (as this maze is ordinarily used) than they did into the entry box. Analysis of the individual records suggests that this is in very large part, if not wholly, attributable to two factors: First, the rats were inserted into the maze at the third cul, and pursuing a straight-ahead course out of this cul leads the animal to the latter half of the maze. Secondly, the maze pattern immediately preceding the goal box is clearly such, as is shown by an analysis of the first runs of 75 rats previously used in this maze, that even the wholly *naive* animal tends to make the turn into the goal box rather than into the cul at his first exposure to this choice point. It is, we think, unlikely that there were food odors lingering from previous experiments; no food had ever been spilled on the wood, and the maze had been washed prior to these runs.

EXPERIMENT II

Because these results might be suspect due to the apparently greater attractiveness of the goal box than of the cul, a second experiment was performed.

Method

Eight male albino rats, experimentally naive, were used. The procedure here was similar to that of Experiment I except that the animals were on an 8-hr. hunger drive, and the two exploratory sessions were only 15 min. each. Rats were introduced at the choice points of culs 2, 3, *or* 5, but not at the same place on both days. They were removed as before, never from the goal or entrance stem, nor from the same place on both days. The major modification was in the test run, which differed from that of Experiment I in that the rats were introduced at the *goal* box and the task was to run the maze *backward*. It seems reasonable to preserve the usage of the word "backward" in this case, since this direction of running a multiple T-maze involves a choice between running straight ahead or turning, although, of course, neither starting nor end box is favored as a "goal" for these rats. In the statistical analyses that follow, then, "backward-going" choices will be considered where appropriate.

Results

The proportion of cul entries per choice for pooled data of all rats is shown in Table 1.

TABLE 1

Proportion of cul entries per opportunity for pooled data from all rats (Experiment II)

	Day 1	Day 2	Test
All cul entries (in first 5 min. for days 1 & 2)	.456	.336	.319
"Backward" errors 1st exposure	.553	.174	.292
All "backward" (in first 5 min. for day 1)	.537		.329

If, instead of pooling data of all rats, as in Table 1, we calculate the significance of reductions in the ratio of cul entries per choice (i.e., the significance of the "gains") made by each rat according to several criteria, we observe that:

1. If all approaches to a choice point (either direction, including retracing) are counted, the reduction between exploration days 1 and 2 is significant at <.02 level; the reduction between all of day 1 and the test trial is significant at <.05 level; the reduction between first 5 min. of day 1 and the test trial is significant at <.01 level.

2. For backward-going errors only, the reduction between day 1 and the test is significant at <.01 level.

3. If only *first-exposure* backward-going errors are counted, the reductions between day 1 and day 2, and between day 1 and the test trial, are both significant at <.01 level.

4. The reduction of the ratio of errors made per unit distance traversed between the first 5 min. of day 1 and the test trial is also significant at <.01.

Although we had taken precautions to avoid any

possibility of the usual reinforcements at removal, we felt it would be particularly striking to show cul elimination within the first free exploration period, since the rats could not by any stretch of the imagination be thought of as having received any but an immediate, intra-maze reward or punishment. Any reinforcing effect due to "removal from constraint of maze" or "return to home cage" would have had no chance to occur in connection with any response or maze locus. The differences in "error-likelihood" among rats and among units make statistical treatment difficult, and only one among several analyses will be suggested here. For each rat, a table was set up showing for his successive exposures to each unit (distinguishing direction of approach), the depth of cul entry (0, 1, 2, or 3, a 3 signifying a cul entry to the very end). For a given unit, the depths of penetration on successive exposures could be summoned to give the *total* (not mean!) *penetration into that unit* (by that rat) up to any given choice. Inspection of this table shows that, in general, when a rat has made considerable previous penetrations into a given unit, he is less likely to enter it, or if he enters, to penetrate it deeply, than when he has not previously penetrated it so deeply, or frequently, or both. A *t*-test shows that this effect is significant at the .01 level.

EXPERIMENT III

Because of the small number of rats and borderline results in the first experiment, and the somewhat ambiguous status of the "choice" when running backward, as in the second, we have tested for this effect a third time, conducting the test runs in a "forward" direction as in Experiment I.

Method

Ten male albino rats, experimentally naive, were used. The same maze was used as in Experiments I and II. The exploration took place during three 15-min. periods on three successive days. Points of removal were recorded and showed this time a good distribution over the maze for every rat. There was no tendency at all to prefer the goal or entry box or to spend more time in one half of the maze than in the other.

Results

The distribution of first forward-going error scores for the ten rats on their test run was: 0, 0, 0, 2, 2, 2, 2, 3, 3, 4.

Comparing the results of the test trial against chance: first-exposure forward-going errors, all forward-going errors, and all choices are significantly less than chance at the <.01 level.

The proportion of cul entries per choice for pooled data from all rats is shown in Table 2.

TABLE 2

Proportion of cul entries per opportunity for pooled data from all rats (Experiment III)

	Day 1	Test
All cul entries (in first 5 min. for day 1)	.563	.253
Forward errors first exposure	.509	.310
All forward (in first 5 min. for day 1)	.515	.289

The analysis of individual rat gains shows that:

1. For all approaches to a choice point, the reduction between day 1 and day 2, and the reduction between day 1 and the test trial are significant at the <.01 level.

2. For forward-going errors only, the reduction between day 1 and test trial yields a p of <.01.

3. If first-exposures, forward-going only, are counted, the reduction between day 1 and day 2 is significant at the <.02 level, but the reduction between day 1 and the test is significant at <.10.

4. The reduction of the ratio of summed weighted errors made per unit distance traversed is significant from day 1 to day 2, and from day 1 to the test trial, at the <.01 level.

DISCUSSION

The data indicate that when special precautions are taken to avoid giving any of the usual kinds of reinforcement, the rat nevertheless shows a significant tendency to "learn" the maze in the sense that when subsequently run in either direction, he tends to avoid the culs. As noted earlier, these data do not make clear what factors produce this learning. It is difficult to conceive of them as being based on anything other than the differential effects of unimpeded running *versus* stopping and turning around. It would be desirable to determine to what extent the preference is based upon some positive reinforcement following a "correct" choice (e.g., exploratory opportunity) and to what extent it is based upon negative reinforcing (anxiety-producing?) consequences of cul entry. We do have unpublished data showing that, in this same maze pattern, but with the alleys 1 in. narrower, the cul elimination in the absence of reinforcement is more pronounced; this suggests that in considerable part the effect is due to the negatively reinforcing aspect of having to turn around in a confined space.

The significance of these results for studies of maze learning, particularly those involving "latent learning" in multiple-unit mazes, is obvious. When there is no food or water reinforcement in the goal box, and even when the various secondary reinforcements involved in removal from the maze and return to the home cage are discounted, *there remain immediate intra-maze consequences of a choice* which favor the elimination of the culs. Any operation which increases the general activity or motivational level could then facilitate the behavioral manifestation of the differential habit strengths thus accumulated.

REFERENCE

1. BLODGETT, H. C. The effect of the introduction of reward upon the maze performance of rats. *Univ. Calif. Publ. Psychol.*, 1929, 4, 113-134.

Part III

8

On the Dual Nature of Learning—A Reinterpretation of "Conditioning" and "Problem Solving"

O. Hobart Mowrer

["*In the psychology of learning, there are three major traditions: hedonism, associationism, and rationalism. Many writers have attempted to base their understanding of learning exclusively upon one or another of these traditions; others have drawn unsystematically from all three. The position taken by the author of the present article is that there are* two basic learning processes—*'conditioning' (associationism) and 'problem solving' (hedonism)—and that rationality is a complex derivative of these other two. However, in order for such a synthesis to be possible, conditioning and problem solving must, the author believes, be defined in the rather special ways here proposed.*

"*If this type of formulation proves valid, it holds promise of not only resolving a number of theoretical paradoxes but of opening the way for new and important applications of the principles of learning in education, clinical work, human relations, and other related fields.*"

These paragraphs are quoted from the editor's introduction to this article as originally published in the Harvard Educational Review (1947).]

Mowrer, initially committed to the utility of the drive reduction hypothesis, chooses to supplement it with the postulation of a two factor theory of learning designed to bring the opposing points of view closer together. This selection is taken from Chapter 9 of *Learning Theory and Personality Dynamics*, Copyright 1950 by The Ronald Press Company. Reprinted by permission.

One of the distinguishing features of science is that it strives for maximal simplicity, parsimony, and consistency in its basic assumptions, whereas common sense is content with complexity, multiplicity, and inconsistency. Folk explanations often take the form of proverbs, which are notorious for their variety, unrelatedness, and mutual contradiction. Scientific explanations by contrast tend to be interrelated, rigorous, and systematic. Whereas common sense has an "explanation" for everything—once it has happened—but lacks general principles with high predictive power, the ways of science often bring its practitioners up short in the face of paradoxes and set problems which those who rely upon a ubiquitous eclecticism do not encounter.

The history of scientific learning theory, though brief, reflects some of the best traditions in scientific method. In America, William James was the first great writer in this field, and for him *repetition* was "the great law of habit." His student, E. L. Thorndike, found it impossible to make the law of repetition (or "use") account for all his experimental findings and posited the *law of effect* in addition. John B. Watson accepted the law of repetition (or "frequency") but rejected *effect* in favor of *recency*. At a somewhat later stage he came under the sway of Pavlovian thought and concluded that the *conditioned response* was the "fundamental unit of habit."

That these pioneer investigators have been in disagreement concerning their basic hypotheses has sometimes been allowed to overshadow the more important fact that they were all following the behest of science, that one's basic assumptions be explicit, simple, and, if possible, few in number. The wealth of experimental fact which has been accumulated during the past half-century as a result of the systematic formulations and logical deductions of these writers abundantly testifies to the value of this method.

During this period still other hypotheses concerning the learning process have been put forward, explicitly by Gestalt psychology, for example, and by psychoanalysis implicitly; but these hypotheses have not readily lent themselves either to precise experimentation or to rigorous logical analysis and may therefore be dismissed from further consideration at this time.[1]

Within the past two decades there have been no major innovations in basic learning theory, but many investigators have vigorously pursued the implications and possible relatedness of the various fundamental concepts which were formulated during the first and second decades of the century. The last and in many respects most ambitious attempt to base a psychology of learning exclusively upon the principle of conditioning was made by E. B. Holt (1931). While it is uniformly conceded that there is something real and important about the conditioning concept, it is now generally acknowledged that it does not provide a comprehensive learning theory. In the hands of E. R. Guthrie (1935), the principle of recency has received its most vigorous and able exploitation, but O'Connor (1946) has pointed out what would seem to be a fatal defect in this type of theory. The principle of repetition (use, exercise, frequency) has come in for a bombardment of criticism from many sides and is today perhaps the least important of the historically notable concepts in the field. By contrast, the law of effect, which was for a long time "an unpopular doctrine" (Thorndike, 1931, p. 33), has stood up exceedingly well and is today probably more influential than any other single conception of the learning process.

For a number of years the present writer and a small group of colleagues and students have attempted to push the law of effect as hard and as far as possible in an effort to determine the full extent of its potentialities—and its limitations, if any. For a time it looked as if this law were indeed *the* basic law of learning, from which all seemingly divergent types of learning could be derived. This view was tentatively suggested by the writer in 1938 (1938c) and has been more confidently proposed in a series of later papers. McGeoch, in *The psy-*

[1] The writer has recently discussed some of the implications of Gestalt psychology for scientific learning theory in an article entitled "The law of effect and ego psychology." For a discussion of psychoanalysis in this connection, see "Time as a determinant in integrative learning."

chology of human learning (1942), has taken a similar position; and numerous other writers have subscribed to this view in varying degree. But it remained for Hull in his *Principles of behavior* (1943), to make the first thoroughgoing attempt to make effect theory serve all purposes.[2]

The purpose of the present paper is to adduce evidence for believing that the law of effect is not valid as a *universal* principle of learning and that it has to be ranged alongside of a second, and independent, type of learning.

I. ASSOCIATION OR EFFECT?

In 1934 Schlosberg published the first of a series of papers, by himself and others, which were designed to determine whether the type of learning which had become known as "conditioning" does or does not obey the law of effect. It had long been known, from the work of Thorndike and many others, that, at least under certain circumstances, responses which "solve problems," i.e., which get "rewarded," are reinforced and that those which "make problems," i.e., which get "punished," are inhibited. In other words, it is well established that in at least some situations responses are strengthened or inhibited according to their *effects*. The question, in simplest form, which Schlosberg and subsequent investigators set out to answer was, therefore, whether conditioned responses, so-called, are likewise influenced by their effects or are governed by some other principle.

The nature and results of Schlosberg's first experi-

[2] It is debatable whether Thorndike can be said ever to have adopted this monistic conception of the learning process. In 1931, he wrote: "Repetition of a connection in the sense of the mere sequence of the two things in time has then very, very little power, perhaps none, as a cause of learning" (pp. 28-29). This might seem to constitute a repudiation of the law of exercise and an endorsement of the law of effect as the sole principle of learning. But in the next sentence he adds, "Belonging is necessary." Moreover, in later publications Thorndike (1943, 1946) has continued to speak as if exercise and effect were both valid principles (cf. later discussion of Thorndike on exercise and effect).

mental approach to this problem are summarized by him as follows:

> In various [earlier] experiments utilizing shock as the unconditioned stimulus, two fundamentally different methods of administering the shock have been utilized. The first method involves the presentation of a shock of predetermined duration, regardless of the response made to the [immediately preceding] conditioned stimulus. In the second method the animal is arranged so that its response will either prevent or terminate the shock. Both methods have been used extensively [by others], apparently without any suggestion that they may be fundamentally different.
>
> [In the present experiment, one group of rats] were always stimulated [following the presentation of the signal] by a shock of 165-sigma [0.165 second] duration. [Another group of rats] were attached to the short-circuiting contacts described above, so that the first millimeter of tail withdrawal would terminate or prevent the shock, and keep it "shorted" until a movement in the reverse direction started. There is no significant difference between the results obtained from the animals that actually shortened the duration of [or avoided] the shock by every response made to it [or to the warning signal], and those that were always given a shock of predetermined duration. This result was very surprising to the writer (p. 322).

The results of this study seem quite unambiguous. They suggest that conditioning is a form of learning that is wholly dependent upon the paired presentation ("association") of two stimulus events, the conditioned stimulus and the unconditioned stimulus, and that it is wholly independent of and unrelated to that form of learning which is known to be dependent upon effect.

The following year, in 1935, Hunter (1935a) published a paper reporting experimental findings which seemed to have implications just the reverse of those of Schlosberg. Rats were again used as subjects, and the nature of the problem under investigation was much the same, but the experimental situation was different. Individually, the subjects were placed on a large circular grill (with appropriate sides and top) consisting of eight sections which could be independently energized by electric shock. At intervals of 1 minute a buzzer was sounded for 2 seconds. With one group of subjects, the presentation of the buzzer was invariably followed by an electric shock which was applied to whatever section of the grill the subject happened to be on at the moment. The shock was applied without regard to whether the subject had or had not moved on the grill in response to the conditioned stimulus. With the other group of subjects the buzzer was followed by shock only if the subject failed to respond to the buzzer by moving to another section of the grill, i.e., failed to make a "conditioned response." In other words, with the second group of subjects a conditioned response, so-called, was effective as a means of avoiding electric shock, whereas in the first group it was ineffective. Hunter comments upon his results as follows:

> Under the conditions of the present experiment, . . . there is a great superiority in the method of not giving the unconditioned stimulus if the conditioned response has been made (p. 144).
>
> Conditioning is quicker on the average if the unconditioned stimulus, shock, is not given after the conditioned response has been made. For ordinary purposes it is suggested that the conditioned and unconditioned stimuli should not always be paired; but that where the subject responds to the conditioned stimulus, the unconditioned stimulus should not be given because of its inhibitory effect upon previously occurring responses (p. 148).

The results thus obtained seem clearly to support the view that conditioning is dependent, not so much upon the paired presentation of the conditioned and unconditioned stimulus, as upon the *effect* produced by the conditioned response: if this response results in the avoidance of the noxious unconditioned stimulus, it will be more readily learned than if it has no such favorable, "problem-solving" consequence.

The year following the publication of Hunter's experiment, Schlosberg published a second paper (1936) in which the same problem was again attacked, with the same general procedure and with the same type of subject as used in his first study, but with the unconditioned stimulus now applied to the rat's leg rather than to the tail. Of his results the author says:

> In the experiments with the tail withdrawal it was found consistently that it made little or no difference in the rate of conditioning whether or not the rat could terminate or avoid the shock by withdrawing the tail. In the present experiments one rat of every experimental pair was trained with short-circuiting contacts arranged so that the first movement [of the leg] shorted the shock, while his experimental mate was trained without these contacts. An examination of the charts will show that the only pair of rats in which there was a clear difference in incidence of leg responses [to the conditioned stimulus] was the pair used in experiment I. In this experiment it was the *noSC* [no short circuit] rat that developed the leg withdrawal, despite the fact that the response did not terminate or prevent the shock. We thus find no more indication that anything comparable to the "law of effect" is working in the conditioned leg reaction than we did for the conditioned tail reaction. . . . In other words, success in avoiding the shock led to extinction of response instead of "stamping it in." This would seem to be an example of what Hull has referred to as "the dilemma of the conditioned defense reaction" (p. 133).[3]

These findings confirm those reported by Schlosberg in 1934 and seemingly refute those reported by Hunter in 1935.

The next major contribution to this problem was reported by Brogden, Lipman, and Culler in 1938.

> Eight guinea pigs were prepared in the rotator, a modified activity-cage which has been found useful in conditioning small animals. Four of the animals (comprising Group A) were trained by the methods commonly employed in this laboratory; that is, the *US* (shock) occurs after *CS* (100-cycle tone) has continued just two seconds. The rotator is so devised that the animals, upon turning the cage an inch or more when the sound begins, escapes [avoids] the shock by breaking the high-voltage circuit through a pendulum. . . . Those [animals] of Group *B*, though exposed to the same situation (same sound, same shock, same test environment), were not allowed to escape [or avoid] the punishment by reacting; on the contrary, each stimulus presentation was reinforced with shock, whether the animal turned the cage or not (pp. 109-10).

[3] This dilemma will be considered later in a different context.

In Group *A*, all subjects were soon making the prescribed response to the conditioned stimulus, and thus avoided the shock on 100 per cent of the trials, whereas the animals in Group *B* never made such a response on more than 50 per cent of the trials. Here, it seemed, was particularly dramatic proof that conditioned responses which are "rewarded," by shock-avoidance, are acquired much more readily than are conditioned responses which are "punished," i.e., followed by shock or some other form of noxious stimulation. On the basis of such evidence it would appear that so-called conditioned responses behave very much as do habitual responses in general, i.e., they obey the law of effect, and do not require any special principle for their explanation.

In the same year, the present writer (1938c) made and briefly reported an attempt to determine whether the galvanic skin response (of human beings) conditions any more readily when it is instrumental in avoiding the noxious stimulus of which the conditioned stimulus is premonitory than when the conditioned G. S. R. has no such effect. The results, as far as the experiment was carried, were inconclusive; but the indications were that the G. S. R. conditions no more rapidly when an instrumental procedure is followed than when the classical procedure is employed. This type of investigation should be repeated, but on the basis of the results obtained there is no basis for believing that the conditioning of the G. S. R. is in any way dependent upon its "effectiveness"; the acquisition of such a conditioned response seems to be wholly a function of the paired presentations of the conditioned and unconditioned stimuli.

But, beginning in 1939, the writer designed and, with the aid of collaborators, carried out a series of experiments, mainly with rats, which seemed to provide increasingly good evidence that so-called conditioned responses are acquired according to and obey precisely the same basic law of learning as do habits in general, namely, the law of effect.

This conclusion was supported by the results of the first experiment in this series in the following way. Using a circular grill very similar to the one previously employed by Hunter, the writer subjected three groups of rats, and later three groups of guinea pigs, to three different experimental conditions. In one group of subjects, a conditioned stimulus (tone) was sounded for 5 seconds at regular minute intervals. If this *CS* elicited a response (a run to an adjacent section of the grill), the shock was omitted. In the second group, exactly the same procedure was followed, save that the trials came at irregular intervals, some of which were as brief as 15 seconds and some as long as 105 seconds, but which *averaged* 1 minute. In the third group, the same procedure was followed as with the first group except that at 15-second intervals during the minute-interval between trials the subject received a shock (without tone) and was forced to run to the adjacent section of the grill.

The findings were that the Group I animals conditioned very satisfactorily and that the Group II and Group III animals conditioned much less satisfactorily. These findings seemed to imply that when the interval between trials was of regular duration and free from disturbance, the satisfaction experienced by the subjects as a result of avoiding the shock which had previously been paired with the conditioned stimulus was greater than when the interval between trials was of irregular duration or when filled with disturbing events, i.e., recurrent electric shocks.[4]

It had previously been taken for granted by various writers that it is in some manner rewarding to an experimental subject to *avoid* a noxious unconditioned stimulus. It is easily seen that it is rewarding to *escape* from such a noxious stimulus. But how can a shock which is *not experienced*, i.e., which is avoided, be said to provide either a source of motivation or of satisfaction? [5] Obvi-

[4] This interpretation is in keeping with Schlosberg's (1934) earlier finding that he could not obtain conditioning in rats when "double stimulation," i.e., conditioning trials, came at the rate of 1 every 9 seconds. When the rate of presentation was reduced to 1 trial every 72 seconds, conditioning was obtained.

[5] In a recent study by Whatmore, Morgan, and Kleitman (1945-46), this problem has been expressed as follows: Having found that dogs acquire a leg-flexion response more readily with an avoidance (instrumental) conditioning procedure than with a nonavoidance (classical) procedure, they say: "We find it

ously the factor of fear has to be brought into such an analysis. *Fear* of electric shock, when aroused by a warning signal, can motivate living organisms, and reduction of such a state can powerfully reward them. Presumably the results just cited were obtained because, in the Group I procedure (free, regular intertrial intervals), the amount of fear reduction, or relief, which was experienced when a conditioned response was made was relatively great, whereas in Groups II and III (irregular, filled intertrial intervals), the amount of fear reduction experienced when a conditioned response was made was relatively slight.

It would thus appear that conditioned avoidance reactions are acquired readily or less readily, depending upon whether they are followed by a "satisfying state of affairs" or by an "annoying state of affairs." If earlier investigators have used primary drives, such as hunger and thirst, to the exclusion of the secondary drives, such as fear, in their study of the law of effect, this, it would seem, is an historical accident. Conditioned responses, so-called, are apparently merely those responses which are acquired as solutions to the problems presented by secondary drives, and as such are quite as much controlled by the law of effect as are other problem-solving responses.

This inference was confirmed by an experiment reported by Mowrer and Lamoreaux in 1942. In this experiment it was found that if the conditioned stimulus (a buzzer) was terminated the instant that the subjects (rats) made a conditioned response (a brief run, to the opposite end of the apparatus, Mowrer and Miller, 1942), reliably better conditioning was obtained than if the

---

difficult at the present time to explain why the avoidance conditioning procedure should work so well at lowering pathway resistances. Some type of reinforcing agent is necessary to maintain performance on the usual type of conditioning, but in avoidance conditioning we can find no such reinforcement. A possible explanation is that the dog is capable of some crude sort of thinking which enables it to realize that by lifting its paw it avoids an unpleasant sensation. It must be aware of the existence of something that it is not experiencing" (pp. 434-35). It is believed that the type of theoretical analysis developed in this paper resolves this paradox.

conditioned stimulus was of arbitrarily fixed duration. The implication of this finding seemed clearly to be that the conditioned stimulus aroused fear and that when the so-called conditioned response occurred and the buzzer was immediately turned off, there was a corresponding reduction in fear which provided a "satisfying state of affairs" and thus reinforced the conditioned response more powerfully than did the termination of the CS (and the attendant reduction of fear) if it either preceded or followed the response by an appreciable length of time. From previous work on the "gradient of reinforcement," we know that a reward which precisely coincides with a given response reinforces that response more than does the same reward when there is an interval (either "forward" or "backward") between the reward and the response. The results obtained in the experiment just described indicate unmistakably that the termination of the buzzer provided a rewarding state of affairs and that this state of affairs was highly significant in determining the strength of the so-called conditioned response of running.

Additional evidence of the problem-solving nature of conditioned responses was forthcoming from a second experiment by Mowrer and Lamoreaux, published in 1946. If conditioning is merely a matter of associative learning in the sense that one stimulus becomes able to do the "work" of another one, i.e., elicit the same response, it might be expected that a so-called conditioned response would always be an exact replica of its unconditioned prototype. Yet the fact is that so-called conditioned responses often differ considerably from their prototypes.[6] If, on the other hand, a conditioned response is the solution to a secondary drive or "problem," such as fear, then it might be expected that that response will be "conditioned" which provides the best solution to this problem, regardless of whether it is the same as or different from the response made to the situation from which the secondary drive has been derived. Thus, it seemed possible that, for example, a rat which had learned to *escape* from an electric shock by running might learn to *avoid* the shock by jumping or

[6] This problem will be considered again on a later page.

doing something else radically different from running, provided only that this other response caused the danger signal to cease and the attendant fear to be reduced.[7]

Suffice it to say here that, in the experiment cited, this prediction was well confirmed. It was found possible to produce so-called conditioned responses, i.e., responses to a danger signal, which were as different as imaginable from the responses which the subjects regularly made to the pain-stimulus of which the danger signal forewarned. This finding cannot easily, if at all, be explained solely on the basis of associative theory.

In an unpublished study, Lamoreaux and Mowrer have pushed the problem-solving conception of the so-called conditioning process one step further, identifying it with learning, or habit-formation, in general. In a study made earlier, it had been pointed out that salivary conditioning as described by Pavlov can be interpreted simply as a matter of discrimination learning; and it now appeared that avoidance conditioning, which may at first seem to represent conditioning in purest form, might also be conceived in a similar fashion. It has been common practice to speak as if the conditioned stimulus in the Pavlovian type of experiment becomes the sole and sufficient cause of the salivary reaction which it elicits. Actually, it has long been known that the subject must also be *hungry* and must, as a rule, be in the *same situation* as the one in which food (the so-called unconditioned stimulus) has previously been received. Viewed in this light, the conditioning process may easily be interpreted as a process of discrimination, in which the subject learns to differentiate between hunger-situation-and-CS (to which it is appropriate to salivate) and hunger-situation-and-no-CS (to which it is not appropriate to salivate). In other words, the CS, in such experiments, seems to function more as a *cue* than as a *signal*, i.e., it tells the hungry animal *when*

[7] In this way is resolved the question, raised on an earlier page, as to how the avoidance of shock can be rewarding. The fact seems to be that the *avoidance* of shock, or any other painful experience, is never, in and of itself, rewarding. The reward comes when the fear of such an experience is reduced or, still better, eliminated.

to expect food. If the animal were not hungry, the *CS* would not activate it, as, for example, a danger signal would.[8]

By contrast, in an avoidance conditioning experiment, the *CS* seems to be clearly a signal, and it is correspondingly difficult to see how the resulting learning can be thought of as discrimination. However even this difficulty vanishes when one takes into account a phenomenon which previous investigators have more or less systematically neglected. After a few paired presentations of the conditioned and unconditioned stimuli in an avoidance experiment, the response which is originally elicited exclusively by the unconditioned stimulus begins to occur, not only to the conditioned stimulus, or signal, but also between trials, "to the situation." These latter responses are commonly referred to as "spontaneous," or "interval," response, and are usually regarded as an uninteresting nuisance, to be minimized if possible and, if not, ignored.

Even the most superficial observation suggests that these interval responses occur because the subject is *afraid*, not only of the discrete stimulus, which has been associated with the *UnCS*, but also of the *whole experimental situation*. Therefore, the so-called conditioning which occurs in experiments of this kind, i.e., the process whereby the *CS* becomes increasingly efficient as an instigator of the responses in question, may well be thought of simply as a process whereby the subject learns that experimental-situation-without-*CS* is safe, whereas experimental-situation-with-*CS* is dangerous. As this kind of "cognitive restructuring" takes place, the interval responses, which are useless, disappear and the conditioned responses, which are useful, appear with mounting regularity.

In the study under discussion, the results were entirely consistent with this interpretation: when it was easy for the subjects to differentiate between the dangerous and the safe periods, "conditioning" proceeded rapidly: when it was difficult so to differentiate (due to special experi-

[8] In keeping with this interpretation is the fact that in the early stages of such training a dog will salivate between the trials, showing that it has not yet clearly differentiated between situation-without-*CS* and situation-with-*CS*.

mental conditions which cannot here be described), "conditioning" proceeded slowly.

Thus it came about, through the series of experiments just described, that even the avoidance response, which has often been assumed to typify conditioning in purest form, is reducible to an instance of simple problem-solving behavior, or habit formation.

Some years ago Thorndike (1931) remarked:

> I must admit that the reported phenomena of the conditioned reflex are a mystery to me in many respects. Just what their relation to ordinary learning is I do not know, but I am not convinced that they show its fundamental pattern and most general principles (p. 113).

More recently Morris (1946) in the concluding pages of his book, *Signs, language, and behavior*, has referred to "the great vagueness in the term 'conditioned response' " (p. 309).

Other investigators, on independent grounds, have thus arrived at the same conclusion as that toward which the foregoing series of experiments seems to point, namely, that "conditioning" is an ill-defined concept, that the phenomena subsumed under it are not fundamentally different from "habits" in general, and that the concept is more misleading than useful and may profitably be dropped.[9]

II. ASSOCIATION AND EFFECT

Since science strives for parsimony in its basic assumptions, it is understandable that attempts should have been made to account for all learning solely in terms of the law of effect. While acknowledging the molar differences between "habits" and so-called conditioned responses, a number of writers have attempted to account

[9] It is interesting to examine Hilgard and Marquis' highly useful book, *Conditioning and learning* (1940), in this connection. Although the term "conditioning" is used in the title in such a way as to suggest that it is something different from "learning," the reader discovers that in the text itself these two terms are used as if they were more or less synonymous. Cf. later discussion of "instrumental" conditioning.

for both as instances of the same fundamental learning process.

In 1938 the present writer (1938c) made such an attempt, as follows:

> Just as incidental . . . stimuli which are temporally contiguous with those responses which are made at the time of escape from hunger, for example, become integrated with the hunger stimulus into a total stimulus pattern which, with repetition, becomes more and more specifically connected with these responses, so would it appear that stimuli which are temporally contiguous with those responses which occur at the time of escape from an anticipatory tension [e.g., fear] likewise become integrated with the anticipatory tension into a total stimulus pattern which, with repetition, becomes likewise more and more specifically connected with these responses. Eventually such incidental stimuli may acquire sufficient excitatory value as to be capable alone of eliciting the responses with which they have been temporarily associated, without the accompanying presence of the original motivating stimuli (pp. 73-74).

In 1942 Mowrer and Lamoreaux (4) attempted to make this hypothesis more explicit by distinguishing between "parasitic" reinforcement and "intrinsic" reinforcement. "Parasitic" reinforcement is here used to designate the strengthening of the tone-running (conditioned) sequence through the action of the basic rewarding situation provided by the shock termination. The strengthening of the shock-running (trial-and-error) sequence may, in contradistinction, be termed "intrinsic reinforcement" (pp. 3-4). It was here again assumed that there was only one basic reinforcing process, namely, that which occurs when a drive is reduced, a problem solved.

The concept of "redintegration," which is very likely to be suggested to the reader by the foregoing quotations, is, of course, an old one. However, in these quotations the attempt is made to make redintegrative, or associative, learning dependent upon the law of effect, rather than to explain it in terms of a separate principle, as has been the common practice.

In Hull's 1943 book, *Principles of behavior,* there appears a section entitled "The conditioned reflex as a special case of ordinary learning reinforcement," in which the author develops the same monistic conception of learning.[10] He says:

> Because of the current differences of opinion concerning the relationships between selective learning and conditioned-reflex learning, an explicit and somewhat detailed comparison of them as types will be made. . . . [Illustrative examples] suggest that the differences between the two forms of learning are superficial in nature; i.e., that they do not involve differences in the conditions under which the principle operates. . . . On one critical point both cases are identical—the reinforcing state of affairs in each consists in the abolition of the shock-injury or need, together with the associated decrement in the drive and drive receptor impulse, at once after the temporal conjunction of the afferent receptor discharge and the reaction. This is, of course, all in exact conformity with the law of primary reinforcement formulated above. . . .
>
> Pavlov differs from the law of reinforcement by regarding as the critical element of the reinforcing state of affairs the occurrence of S_u, in this case the *onset* of the shock. On the other hand, the critical element in the reinforcing state of affairs by our own hypothesis is the reduction in the drive receptor impulse which accompanies the reduction of the need, i.e., reduction of the physiological injury of the feet, caused by the termination of the shock . . .
>
> It is an easy matter to show the inadequacy of Pavlov's formulation as a general theory of learning. . . . It is not difficult to understand how Pavlov could have made such an error. His mistaken induction was presumably due in part to the exceedingly limited type of experiment which he employed (pp. 76-79).

Figure 45 presents these two theories of reinforcement diagrammatically. Each of these theories accounts well enough for those instances in which the response elicited by the *CS* is an exact replica of the response elicited by the *UnSC;* but a theory of conditioning must also be able to explain those instances in which the so-called conditioned response differs radically from

[10] Cf. a series of papers by Youtz (1938a, 1938b, 1939) in which a number of seeming parallels between "Pavlovian" and "Thorndikian" learning are adduced. See also an earlier (1927) paper by Symonds.

the unconditioned response, as, for example, in the experiment by Mowrer and Lamoreaux (5), previously described. Such results can be made intelligible only if fear is posited as an intervening variable (cf. Tolman, 1932), and neither Pavlov's nor Hull's type of analysis has any place in it for such an intermediate factor. What clearly happens when a CS is paired with a noxious *UnCS* is that the CS becomes a danger signal and arouses fear, and it is the fear which then serves to motivate the externally observed defensive behavior. The latter seems to be largely determined by effect learning and may be like or quite unlike the overt behavior aroused by the original noxious drive.

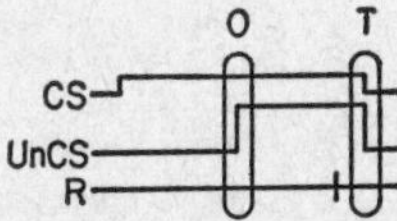

Fig. 45. Diagram illustrating two theories of conditioning. According to Pavlov, reaction R *becomes connected with the conditioned stimulus,* CS, *because of what happens at* O. *According to Hull, reaction* R *becomes connected with the* CS *because of what happens at* T. *For Pavlov it is the contiguity of the* CS *and the* onset *of the* UnCS *that is crucial, whereas for Hull it is the contiguity of the* CS *and the* termination *of the* UnCS *that is all-important. In this illustration, the* UnCS *may be thought of as any noxious stimulus, such as an electric shock, and the* CS *as any innocuous stimuli, such as a tone or a light.*

Having established this much, the question which now arises is: How is fear learned? Is it acquired on the basis of what happens at O or at *T* (Figure 45)? If Pavlov had ever interested himself in the phenomenon of fear, he would presumably have said that it becomes attached to the *CS* by virtue of the mere conjunction of the *CS* and the *UnCS*. Hull's theory, on the other hand, would lead us to expect that the fear would become attached to the *CS* because of the satisfying state of affairs experienced when the *UnCS* is terminated. The latter expectation is contrary to intuitive common sense and to biological considerations. Why, one asks, should living organisms be so constructed that they can learn to fear traumatic stimulation only when that stimulation is "all over"? Would it not seem preferable for them to be constructed in such a way that fear-learning is produced by the coincidence of a danger signal and the impact of the trauma?

In an experiment which will shortly be reported by Suter, Horton, and Traum, evidence has been obtained which shows that fear-learning is indeed dependent, not upon situation *T* but upon situation O (Figure 45). The logic of this experiment is as follows. If the

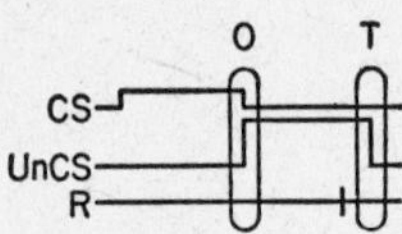

Fig. 46. Diagram of experimental procedure in which the CS *is turned off at* O *instead of being kept on until* T, *as in Figure 45. If the reinforcement of the connection between* CS *and* R *were dependent on what happens at* T, *this connection would be expected to develop less readily with this procedure than with the one depicted in Figure 45. The fact that the* CS-R *connection seems to develop just as readily when the* CS *terminates at* O *as when it extends to* T *suggests that for this kind of learning the reinforcement is provided by what happens at* O, *not at* T. *However, this analysis presupposes the division of labor posited in the text between reactions which are mediated by the autonomic nervous system and those mediated by the central nervous system. No attempt is made either in Figure 45 or in Figure 46 to indicate this relatively complex relationship.*

capacity of the CS to become a danger signal is dependent upon its coincidence with the termination of the *Un*CS, then the CS should become more ominous to the subject if it overlaps and terminates with the *Un*CS than if the CS does not overlap with the *Un*CS, as shown in Figure 46. It is not possible here to give all the details of this experiment; but the important fact for the present purposes is that the above prediction is not confirmed: there even appears to be a slight tendency for the CS to become more ominous to the subject if the CS and the *Un*CS do *not* overlap.

No one will gainsay the importance and legitimacy of the attempt to derive a single, monistic principle of learning. For the teacher of learning theory no less than for the investigator, it would be very convenient if learning were a simple, unitary process. But the fact seems to be that learning is a more complicated procedure, and it is unrealistic to try to adduce a theory which does not appropriately acknowledge this complexity. We know that, in certain instances of learning, what happens when a drive is terminated and satisfaction is experienced is crucially important; but it now appears equally clear that certain other instances of learning depend upon the onset, rather than upon the termination, of a drive. Some other principle which is quite different from either the law of effect or the principle of association may ultimately make possible a unified theory of the reinforcement process; but for the present it seems necessary to assume that there are *two basic learning processes:* the process whereby the solutions to problems, i.e., ordinary "habits," are acquired; and the process whereby emotional learning, or "conditioning," takes place.[11]

[11] This conclusion has been forced upon the writer, not only by the experimental findings which are reviewed in this and the preceding section, but also by some particularly cogent and forceful criticisms which Professors P. B. Rice (1946) and G. W. Allport (1946) have recently directed against the author's earlier view that "living organisms learn when and only when they solve a problem in the sense of reducing a tension, relieving a discomfort, deriving a satisfaction" (8, p. 210). Although convinced of the validity and importance of the law of effect, Rice prefers "to leave it an open question whether the law of effect can be taken as the sole principle of learning, or whether a law of exercise is also needed, perhaps together with still other principles." "It is hard to see how mere exercise or repetition, without satisfaction or need-reduction, could fail to have some effect on the associative neural tracts, even though this effect may be slighter than the 'retroflex' action of reward" (p. 309). And Allport, while accepting effect as a secondary principle of learning, maintains that "effect cannot possibly be the *only* law of learning" (p. 338) and remarks that it is easy "to demonstrate that learning takes place when no drives have been reduced. Suppose while using a cleaning fluid I am careless with a match. . . . Suppose I

This distinction, because it employs the term "conditioning," in a much more restricted and rigorous sense than has been common practice, immediately requires a word of explanation. As we have seen in the preceding section, the broader and more customary usage applies the term "conditioning" to the acquisition of any response which occurs to a signal or CS of any kind. This usage has broken down on both logical and pragmatic grounds and should be discontinued. As we have seen, many *so-called* conditioned responses are simply solutions to secondary-drive problems and are learned in the same way as are problem solutions in general, i.e., through trial-and-error and the law of effect.[12] But it is also apparent that the law of effect is not adequate to account for the process whereby these secondary drives are themselves acquired; and it is for this latter process, exclusively, that the term "conditioning" should be reserved.

Such a procedure has a number of advantages which will be reviewed in a later section; first, however, it will be useful to note certain other justifications for using

---

mispronounce a word in a public speech . . . and suffer mounting shame and discomfort. Tension has been *created*, not reduced; *dissatisfaction* and not satisfaction has resulted; but in this sequence of events I shall surely learn" (p. 342). These criticisms are well taken, and it is hoped that the point of view presented in the present paper will meet them, but will, at the same time, avoid the manifest difficulties which multiple-principle learning theories have previously encountered (cf., for example, the later discussion of Thorndike's principles of effect and exercise).

[12] In earlier publications the author has stressed the usefulness of the distinction which Hilgard and Marquis (1940) have drawn between the "classical" conditioning procedure (invariable pairing of *CS* and *UnCS*) and the "instrumental" conditioning procedure (paring of *CS* and*UnCS* only when the *CS* does not elicit the expected response). An "instrumental conditioned response" now appears to be a contradiction in terms. Only *skeletal* responses are instrumental in the sense of performing "work," producing "results," changing the external world; and if the term "conditioning" is to be restricted, as now seems desirable, to the process whereby responses of the smooth muscles and glands are acquired, it is clearly inappropriate to speak of a conditioned response as instrumental. This point will be returned to on a later page.

the term "conditioning" in this, and only this, sense and for making the conditioning process separate and distinct from the learning process denoted by the law of effect.

III. COLLATERAL SUPPORT FOR A TWO-FACTOR THEORY OF LEARNING

There are reasons other than that of conceptual convenience for supposing that there are two distinctive learning processes. In stressing the "unity of the individual," or the "organism as a whole," we are likely to gloss over the fact that in all mammals and in many other phyla the individual organism is divided into two great response systems, that of the *skeletal muscles* and that of the *smooth muscle* and *glands*. The responses mediated by the latter are appropriately termed *physiological*, whereas those mediated by the former are *behavioral* in the usual sense of that term. Just as an army must have both its "supply" units and its "action" units, so must the individual organism have organs of supply and organs of action.

The fundamental nature of this dichotomy is further emphasized by the fact that mammals and other complex living organisms have, not "*a* nervous system," but two distinct *nervous systems*. Responses of the skeletal muscles are mediated by the *central nervous system*, whereas responses of the visceral and vascular parts of the organism are mediated by the *autonomic nervous system*. In terms of structure and organization, as well as mode of functioning, these two nervous systems are radically different; and it is by no means unreasonable to suppose that the responses which they mediate are subject to very different learning processes.[13]

[13] If one assumes that effect learning is basic and that conditioning is dependent upon it, then one might expect to find that, phylogenetically and ontogenetically, the central nervous system is laid down first and the autonomic later. Kempf (1918) believes that the autonomic is the primitive nervous system and far older than the central nervous system. Although the central nervous system is now "dominant" in higher organisms, this was presumably not the case at an early stage in organic

As a further parallel to this basic dichotomy we may note the familiar differentiation between *voluntary* and *involuntary* responses. Without exception, the visceral and vascular responses are beyond direct voluntary control, whereas all of the skeletal responses (with the unimportant exception of a few "reflexes") are or may be brought under voluntary control. Under ordinary circumstances, the visceral and vascular responses occur in a smoothly automatic fashion, and serve what Cannon (1932) has called the "homeostatic," or physiological, equilibrium-restoring function. These same responses may, however, be made to occur, not only in response to actual physiological needs, but also in response to conditioned stimuli, or signals, of various kinds. And when the visceral and vascular responses occur on the latter basis, as *anticipatory states,* they *produce,* rather than eliminate, physiological disequilibrium and are consciously experienced as *emotion.* As such, they play enormously important motivational roles, roles so important to the survival of the organism that it is easily understood why the learning of these responses should be automatic, involuntary, distinct from the type of learning whereby ordinary habits are acquired. Biologically, it is clearly necessary that living organisms be equipped with a nervous system which will cause to be fixated those skeletal responses which reduce drives and give pleasure. But it is equally evident that living organisms must also be equipped with another nervous system which will cause emotional responses to be learned, not because they solve problems or give pleasure in any immediate sense, but because without such responses the organism would have slight chance of survival. There are grounds for believing that all emotions (including fear, anger,

---

evolution. And Hewer (1927) has shown that in the human embryo the unstriped musculature develops first, to be followed later by the striped musculature. There is thus converging evidence that the autonomic-physiological system is more primitive than the central-behavioral system. From this it may seem to follow that conditioning is the basic form of learning and effect learning a "secondary form" (as Allport has proposed, Footnote 11). Whether such an inference is justifiable, on the basis of present knowledge, is uncertain.

and the appetites) are basically painful (i.e., all have drive quality); and it is hard to see how they could be acquired by the same mechanism which fixes those responses (of the skeletal musculature) which are problem solving, drive reducing, pleasure giving. The latter are learned when a problem is resolved, ended; whereas it is often necessary that emotional responses become conditioned to signals which are associated with the *onset*, not the termination, of a problem.[14]

Another way of making the same point is to note (as one of the author's students, Mr. C. G. Chmielenski, has recently done) that trial-and-error learning is parallel to what Freud (1911) has called the *pleasure principle*, whereas conditioning is more closely related to the *reality principle*. In other words, living organisms acquire conditioned responses, or emotions, not because it is pleasant to do so, but because it is *realistic*. It is certainly not pleasant to be afraid, for example, but it is often very helpful, from the standpoint of personal survival (cf. Mowrer and Kluckhohn, 1944, on the distinction between "adjustment" and "adaptation"). At the same time, it is biologically useful for living organisms to be able to learn those responses which reduce their drives, regardless of whether these drives be primary (as in the case of hunger) or secondary (as in the case of fear); but it is apparently quite necessary that the neural mechanism which mediates this kind of learning be different from the mechanism whereby emotional, or "attitudinal," learning comes about.

Nor does the usefulness of differentiating between conditioning and effect learning end here. Anthropolo-

[14] This discussion raises a particularly important, but difficult question: How are appetites learned? Superficially they appear to represent an anticipation of drive reduction, or satisfaction. Thus, for example, salivation (as a physical concomitant of food appetite) may be said to represent an anticipation of hunger reduction. But whether an appetite is learned in the same way as are responses of the skeletal musculature which produce drive reduction, or by the mere pairing of a signal and food (as Pavlov apparently believed) is at present impossible to say. Even less is known about the conditions of anger learning.

gists are tending more and more to define "culture" as accumulated and transmitted problem solutions (Ford, 1939; Kluckhohn and Kelly, 1945; Linton, 1936). However, unless a distinction is immediately made, this definition leads to a serious dilemma; i.e., some items of culture, far from solving problems for the individual in any immediate sense *make* problems for him. This dilemma is quickly resolved if we note that certain items of culture are problem solving primarily, or perhaps exclusively, in the sense of being *individually* useful; whereas certain other items of culture are problem solving primarily, or perhaps exclusively, in the sense of being *socially* necessary. By and large, the solutions to individual problems involve the central nervous system and the skeletal musculature, whereas the solutions to social problems involve the autonomic nervous system and the organs which mediate emotional responses. Intrinsically, it is hardly helpful to the individual to be told, "Thou shalt not do thus and so," but it may be socially very necessary, and, in the long run but not in any immediately discernible psychological sense, also advantageous to the individual.[15]

Similarly, in the field of education it is useful to differentiate between *teaching* and *training*. Teaching may be defined as the process whereby one individual helps another learn to solve a problem more quickly or effectively than would be likely on the basis of that individual's own unaided, trial-and-error efforts. Here we are dealing with "items of culture" which are individually helpful. Training, by contrast, may be thought of as involving learning whose primary objective is social rather than individual. In this connection one naturally thinks of "items of culture" which are associated with such words as "morality," "character," "social responsibility," etc. Such a distinction as the one here proposed between teaching and training is helpful in deciding the oft-debated question as to whether "indoctrination" is a legitimate function of education. It is also relevant to some of the issues which have arisen between

[15] Cf. also Mowrer and Ullman on the distinction between "adjustment" and "integration." See also the concluding paragraphs of the present paper on the "problem of conscience."

Progressive Education and more traditional educational philosophies.[16]

Although current laboratory practice is not completely differentiated in this connection, it may nevertheless be worth noting that the method of plotting "learning curves" tends to be different when trial-and-error learning is involved from what it is when conditioning is involved. What is probably the commonest procedure, in the former instance, is to note and graph the *time required* by the subject to make the "correct" response after the

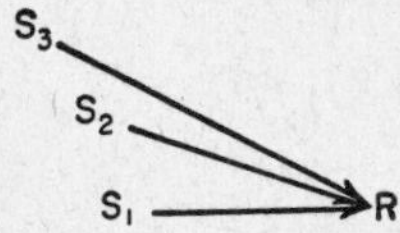

Fig. 47. Diagrammatic representation of conditioning, or stimulus substitution. Originally only S_1 *is capable of producing* R; *but as a result of the contiguous occurrence of* S_2 *and* S_1, S_2 *becomes able to elicit* R. *This change represents "first order" conditioning. And if* R *becomes attached to* S_3 *through the pairing of* S_3 *and* S_2, *this change is referred to as "second order" conditioning. In this type of learning,* R *is a response mediated by the autonomic nervous system.*

"problem" is presented. Learning is thus seen graphically as a descending curve. In the case of conditioning, on the other hand, the usual practice is to note whether a specified response does or does not occur (and possibly to what extent) in response to the so-called "conditioned stimulus." This type of learning is therefore represented graphically as an ascending curve.

An even more explicit difference arises from the fact that conditioning involves what may be termed stimulus substitution whereas problem-solving learning involves response substitution. This contrast is presented diagrammatically in Figures 47 and 48.

In Figure 47, if S_1 is a stimulus which can be relied upon to elicit the emotional response *R*, and if S_2 is

[16] Cf. also Kilpatrick's (1925) discussion of "concomitant" learnings, i.e., the unintentional emotional conditioning which often accompanies supposedly pure "teaching."

presented along with S_1, then S_2 quickly becomes a substitute for S_1. This is commonly known as "first-order" conditioning. But if, after S_2 has become capable of producing the same response as S_1, S_2 is paired with S_2, then S_3 may become capable of eliciting the response in question. This is known as "second order" conditioning. Pavlov (1927) has shown that salivary conditioning in dogs can be carried to the "third order." How far "higher order" conditioning, involving different subjects and different responses, can be carried has not been fully determined. (To the reader who is not accustomed to think in terms of this type of learning, the analogy of the teaching of a foreign language by the "direct" and

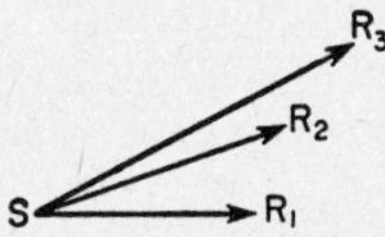

Fig. 48. Diagrammatic representation of problem solving, or response substitution. Originally S *produces* R_1*; but if* R_1 *does not lead to a satisfactory outcome, it is inhibited and* R_2 *occurs. If* R_2 *likewise fails to prove rewarding,* R_3 *occurs. If this latter response "solves the problem," i.e., eliminates* S*, the connection between* S *and* R_3 *is reinforced, and* R_3 *tends to replace both* R_1 *and* R_2 *In this type of learning* R_1, R_2, *and* R_3 *are mediated by the central nervous system.*

"indirect" methods may be useful. The first method corresponds roughly to first-order conditioning and the indirect method to second-order conditioning i.e., in the first case the "word" is associated directly with the "thing," whereas in the second case the "word" is expected to acquire the proper meaning by virtue of association with another "word," rather than with the "thing.")

The diagram shown in Figure 48 represents learning of the problem-solving, or response-substitution, type. If S is a drive, or a "problem situation," the subject's first response, R_1, may not be effective. It is followed by R_2, which may likewise not be effective. R_2 is followed in turn by R_3, which, let us suppose, is effective. On subsequent occasions, when S recurs, R_3 will tend to be the dominant response. It may be said to have become a substitute for R_1.

This distinction between conditioning and problem solving has recently been expressed by Scott (1947) somewhat differently but very explicitly, as follows:

> The behavior of an animal can be divided into two categories: modifiable and nonmodifiable behavior. In the first class falls most of the external behavior. If an animal's first reaction does not produce satisfactory adjustment to stimulation, he can alter it and produce a more satisfactory one. In the second class is most of the internal behavior of an animal, including the secretion of glands and the contractions of smooth muscles. Such activities follow a standard pattern, and while they can be associated with certain stimuli, and thus be affected by learning, the nature of the reaction never varies except in its strength. In this same class of behavior also belong certain types of external behavior which have been usually termed reflexes. It is, of course, this nonmodifiable behavior which has the closest association with the term emotion (p. 279).[17]

That there is a fundamental difference between the two forms of learning which are here designated as conditioning and as problem solving is made clear in yet another way. There have been many experiments and discussions on "the gradient of reinforcement," but if there are two basically different types of reinforcement, one would expect to find *two* gradients of reinforcement. This expectation is well founded. In the gradient of reinforcement of the problem-solving type, the variable that is important is the interval of time between the occurrence of the correct response and the occurrence of the ensuing rewarding state of affairs. If this interval is

[17] This way of dichotomizing the responses of living organisms has the interesting incidental effect of resolving the question. Why do conditioned responses, so-called, sometimes differ from their unconditioned prototypes? The answer is that if the term "conditioned response" is restricted to visceral-vascular responses, the problem disappears, since such responses are always much the same, whether elicited by a *CS* or an *UnCS*. (This is not say, however, that their subjective counterparts are necessarily the same. Cf. the earlier discussion of emotions as physiological preparations.)

short, the reinforcement is great; if the interval is long, then the reinforcement is slight. On the other hand, in the gradient of reinforcement of the conditioning type, the variable that is important is the interval of time between the occurrence of the *CS* and the occurrence of the *UnCS*. If the *CS* precedes the *UnCS* only slightly or actually coincides with it, then the reinforcement is great: but if the interval between the *CS* and the *UnCS* is longer, then the reinforcement is proportionately lessened. We thus arrive at what is one of the most clear-cut distinctions between the two types of learning which are here under discussion.

In summary, then, we see that there are many and highly diverse sources of evidence for the two-factor theory of learning which is here under consideration. Such a theory presupposes a delimitation of the term "conditioning" as it is usually employed and an extension of the traditional concept of "effect" learning. The term "conditioning" has commonly been used, erroneously as it now seems, to denote the process whereby a living organism comes to make any response, skeletal or visceral, immediate or delayed, to a stimulus which has "signal value." As we saw in the preceding section, this usage is too broad for precise scientific purposes. It now seems preferable to apply the term "conditioning" to that and only that type of learning whereby *emotional* (visceral and vascular) responses are acquired. By contrast, effect learning has been previously conceived as applying mainly in those situations in which the motive, or "problem," is an unlearned biological drive, such as hunger, thirst, pain, etc. It is now clear that effect learning must be expanded to include those situations in which the motive, or "problem," is a *learned* drive, that is, an emotion such as fear or an appetite. Many responses involving the skeletal musculature, which have previously been termed "conditioned responses," are, in the present conceptual scheme, not conditioned responses at all. Only those responses which involve visceral and vascular tissue and which are experienced subjectively as emotion are assumed to be conditioned responses. If an emotion, or secondary drive, causes the skeletal musculature to be activated and if such activity results in secondary drive reduction, then the overt response thus acquired is here conceived as an instance of effect learning, not conditioning.

One other matter remains to be considered, although the limitations of both space and precise knowledge are such that it can be considered only in the most general terms. In the foregoing pages we have repeatedly spoken of *two* nervous systems, the central and the autonomic. We must now briefly examine their interrelationship and, in one important respect, the dependence of one upon the other.

Of the two, the central nervous system is the more complete, composed as it is of sensory nerves, internuncial nerves, and motor nerves, by means of which it is possible, at least in principle, for an impulse from any sense organ to be relayed to any part of the skeletal musculature. On the other hand, the autonomic nervous system, strictly speaking, is an exclusively motor, or efferent, system. As Fulton (1943) remarks, "The sympathetic chain and vagus obviously carry many afferent fibres, some sensory in nature, giving rise to visceral pain, and others involved in viscero-visceral and viscero-somatic reflexes that never reach consciousness. There is some question, however, whether such fibres should be classified as 'autonomic,' the term adopted by Langley for a purely efferent outflow, and it is perhaps better to use the standard morphological term 'visceral afferent' " (p. 194). It is obvious, therefore, that communication, if communication there be, between the so-called autonomic nervous system and the sensorium of the individual must be supplied by the sensory pathways of the central nervous system. And the fact that both external and internal stimuli of various kinds may activate the autonomic leaves no doubt that such communication does exist. The question is how and where it is that ordinary sensory impulses, traveling inward on the central nervous system, get shunted onto fibers communicating with the autonomic system.

For an answer we may again turn to Fulton. He says:

> Autonomic nerves . . . are in no way independent of somatic. The two are interdependent. . . . We find somatic and autonomic functions regulated from common levels in

> the cord, brain, stem, hypothalamus and cortex (p. 191). In the cortex there is extensive overlapping between autonomic and somatic motor representation, making possible unified correlation between the reactions of the two systems. In general, the topographical relation between the cortical areas influencing specific autonomic functions is close to the cortical area influencing the corresponding functions. Thus lacrimation is observed on stimulating the eye fields, salivation, on stimulation of the motor representation of the face and tongue (p. 444).

In other words, it is now established that there are numerous "representations" of the autonomic nerves in the most complex parts of the central nervous system, and that from the standpoint of neuroanatomy there is no difficulty in getting an impulse which enters the central nervous system from any sensory organ to discharge through the autonomic system. The structural basis is thus laid for the occurrence of that form of learning which is involved in conditioning; but how this is achieved, functionally, is still a mystery. What is important to note for present purposes is merely that, anatomically, there is just as much basis for assuming that conditioning occurs in the cerebral cortex as for supposing that problem-solving learning occurs there. There is, in other words, no neuroanatomical evidence which argues against the two-factor theory of learning, and there is some such evidence which is at least implicitly supportive of this theory.

Part IV

9

Reward Value of a Non-nutritive Sweet Taste

FRED D. SHEFFIELD AND THORNTON B. ROBY

Institute of Human Relations, Yale University

The purpose of the present experiments was to help answer the question of what constitutes a "reinforcing state of affairs" in instrumental conditioning. One of the most systematic positions on this topic (4) holds that ultimate reduction of a survival need is an essential factor, and a closely related position (5) argues for the necessity of ultimate reduction in a primary drive. However, several studies (3, 6, 1)—and at least one theory of reinforcement (10)—suggest the possibility that a sweet taste is reinforcing regardless of whether it is produced by a nutritive or non-nutritive substance. These previous studies demonstrate that sweet-flavored water is preferred to plain water by rats. They do not demonstrate, however, whether a sweet taste, per se, will operate as a reward in instrumental conditioning, uncomplicated either by a measurement of purely reflexive ingestion or by acquired reward from nutritive sweet-tasting substances. Also previous studies apparently have not related the sweet preference to the hunger state of the animal. The present experiments demonstrate that a non-nutritive sweet-tasting substance functions as a very effective reward in instrumental conditioning. They also demonstrate that the reward value depends on the degree of hunger present.

The "reward" used for instrumental conditioning in rats was a solution of saccharine in water. This sub-

This article originally appeared in the *Journal of Comparative and Physiological Psychology*, 43, 1950, pp. 471-481.

stance produces a sweet taste in humans which is apparently "satisfying" to its many users (chiefly diabetics and those on reducing diets). The non-nutritive nature of saccharine is indicated by the fact that it apparently goes through the mammalian body unchanged chemically, and animals ingesting it do not diminish their food intake (3). Throughout all the present experiments the solution used was 1.30 grams of pure saccharine powder per liter of water. This value was chosen on the basis of a previous investigation of sweet preference (1) as likely to be effective with most rats.

EXPERIMENT I

Purpose

The purpose of Experiment I was to determine whether a position preference in drinking behavior could be established on the basis of saccharine flavored water and whether the preference varied as a function of degree of hunger.

Method

Six albino rats (age about six months at outset of experiment) were kept hungry by restricting their daily diet to eight grams (dry weight) of ground Purina Dog Chow mixed with 10 cc. of water. Six comparable control animals had food available at all times in the form of standard dry Purina Dog Chow pellets. The living cages were equipped at their rear walls with two 100 cc. graduated cylinders about four inches apart which served as water bottles. The cylinders were held in place by standard steel-clip broom holders, which permitted rapid insertion or removal without dripping of the contents. The water was taken by the rat in the usual way—by lapping from the end of a glass tube. The tips were partially sealed to a diameter small enough to prevent any spontaneous dripping. The laboratory was dimly lighted by a shielded 25-watt lamp at all times except when readings were made and when the daily food was given, at which times a bright overhead light was turned on. The procedure was as follows:

1. Two habituation days in the cages with both groups satiated for food and water, followed by a day in which the six experimental animals were not fed.
2. Five days with water in both bottles, hunger-drive regime as indicated in the Method section.
3. Nineteen days of alternate training and testing. On *training* days a saccharine solution (1.30 grams per liter) was on a given side for a given animal, water being on the other side; on the alternate *testing* days water was on both sides. The saccharine side was on the left for half of the animals of each group and on the right for the other half.

Relative consumption of water and saccharine solution: All animals demonstrated rapid acquisition of a preference for drinking the saccharine solution as compared with the water solution on training days. Regardless of the degree of hunger, the proportion—of total liquid consumed—taken from the saccharine bottle jumped to almost 100 per cent during the first training day. The relevant results are shown in table 1.

TABLE 1

Acquisition of drinking from the saccharine side on training days

	MEAN PER CENT FROM SACCHARINE SIDE OUT OF TOTAL INTAKE OF FLUID FROM BOTTLES			
	Preceding day (water in both bottles)	During first 2½ training hours	During first training day	During tenth training day
Hungry	55.2	88.6	98.8	99.5
Satiated	59.5	77.3	95.5	95.8

Table 1 shows that there was a slight preference in both groups for the "saccharine" side prior to the introduction of saccharine, as indicated by the per cent of water intake during the preceding day when there was water in both bottles. During the first 2½ hours with saccharine in one of the bottles, however, there was a decided preference in both groups for drinking from the saccharine bottle, and over the entire first 24 hours with saccharine both groups drank almost exclusively from the saccharine bottle. There was little difference between the first and last day of training.

Whereas there was no important difference between hungry and satiated animals in the *per cent* of total intake from the saccharine bottle, there was a large difference in *absolute* intake. Hungry animals drank far more saccharine solution than satiated animals. This is shown in table 2, which also compares saccharine drinking with water consumption prior to the first training day.

TABLE 2

Effect of hunger on consumption of saccharine solution

	MEAN CCS. FLUID TAKEN				
	From both water bottles before training	From saccharine bottle during training	Diff.	t	df.
Hungry	24.2	205.4	181.2	9.7	5
Satiated	37.8	78.1	40.3	4.8	5
Diff.	−13.6	127.3			
t	3.7	6.0			
df.	10	10			

It can be seen in table 2 that both hungry and satiated rats markedly increased their fluid intake when the saccharine solution was available. Even satiated animals almost doubled their intake, while the hungry animals increased theirs by a factor of almost nine, drinking over two and one-half times as much of the solution as the satiated animals. It will also be noted that hungry animals drank significantly less water than satiated animals during the five control days before the introduction of saccharine. This may well merely reflect the fact that they received 10 cc. of water in their daily ration of Purina mash. If a constant of 10 cc. is added to the mean it becomes 34.2 and does not differ significantly from that of the satiated group. Thus no clear relation of hunger to water intake is in evidence.

Position preference on test days: All animals showed a preference for the "saccharine" side during the nine interspersed test days on which there was plain water in both bottles. However, the transfer of position preference was not complete, that is, while all animals drank the *majority* of their water from the reinforced side they did not attain the 100 per cent level. On the contrary, the transfer to test days reached a maximum on the second test day and declined thereafter. The important trends are shown in table 3.

TABLE 3

Mean per cent of water taken from the "saccharine" side on test days during training

	MEAN PER CENT FROM "SACCHARINE" SIDE				
	Day before training	1st Test day	2nd Test day	3rd Test day	9th Test day
Hungry	55.2	81.1	82.8	76.7	72.8
Satiated	59.5	76.7	80.2	68.0	57.3

It can be seen in table 3 that transfer of the reinforced position to test days with water only increased to the second test day. At this point both hungry and satiated animals showed reliable transfer (p less than .02 in each group). But the transfer began to decline by the third test day and continued downward through the remainder of training. The decline from the second to the last test day was not significant for either group but at least the failure to progress toward 100 per cent preference indicates either that the reinforcing power of the saccharine solution was extinguishing or that some other factor was interfering with complete transfer of the position preference to the test days with water in boh bottles. One such interfering factor might be frustration due to failing to find a sweet taste in the appropriate bottle on test days. Another could be acquisition of a discrimination involving drinking exclusively from the saccharine side on training days and drinking more or less indiscriminately on the test days. The cue for the differential behavior would be presence or absence of a sweet taste. The critical question for the present study was whether or not the sweet taste was losing its reinforcing power as would be the case if it were an acquired reward. Evidence on this question will be considered next.

Did the reinforcing effect extinguish?: Perhaps the most relevant finding on this question has already been

TABLE 4

Possible extinction of saccharine drinking

		DAY OF SACCHARINE TRAINING				
		1st		2nd		10th
Hungry	Mean ccs.	244.7		195.5		194.8
	diff.		49.2		0.7	
	t		4.3		0.1	
	df.		5		5	
Satiated	Mean ccs.	94.7		77.3		74.3
	Diff.		17.4		3.0	
	t		1.6		0.4	
	df.		5		5	

shown in table 1, in which it is obvious that an almost 100 per cent preference for the saccharine side was maintained throughout the training days for all animals. If the decline in preference on test days is due to decline of reinforcing effect, a comparable decline would be expected on training days.

Another relevant source of evidence is the course of saccharine drinking throughout the 10 training days. The finding here was an initial drop in saccharine drinking in both groups, but with little change from the second to the tenth training day. These results are shown in table 4. The table shows a significant drop between the first and second training days in the hungry group. None of the other differences shown is significant although the difference in each case is in the direction of extinction of saccharine drinking.

While the results demonstrate some initial extinction of saccharine drinking, they do not provide a convincing explanation of the failure to achieve 100 per cent transfer of position preference on test days. This preference declined *after* the saccharine drinking stabilized. Moreover, a decline in saccharine drinking is not necessarily an index of a decline in its reinforcing power—it could be acquisition of a tendency not to get too full a stomach. It should be noted that ingestion of 245 ccs. of fluid (the mean for the first day for hungry rats) involves considerable stomach distension in a 350-gram animal. The amount consumed is comparable to a 150-pound man's consuming 13 gallons of fluid in a 24-hour period.[1]

EXPERIMENT II

Purpose

It had originally been expected that if a sweet taste was reinforcing a progressive acquisition of a position preference on test days would have been shown in Experiment I. This expectation was not borne out; instead the animals showed rapid acquisition of a moderate preference, followed by a tendency toward a decline. The results might be interpreted as evidence that the reinforcing effect of a sweet taste was relatively weak and tended to extinguish in the course of the experiment. On the other hand the results can be interpreted as evidence that the animal was frustrated by absence of a sweet taste on test days or that a discrimination was being established such that the animals would try both bottles and drink only from the sweet side if one was sweet, but

[1] The experimenters had no real check on how much of the saccharine solution was actually ingested because the cages had wire mesh floors with sawdust trays underneath. However, in Experiment III, in which drinking was done over solid floor, very little of the saccharine solution taken was found to be spilled on the floor. In any case the measure used was a good index of instrumental tongue movements.

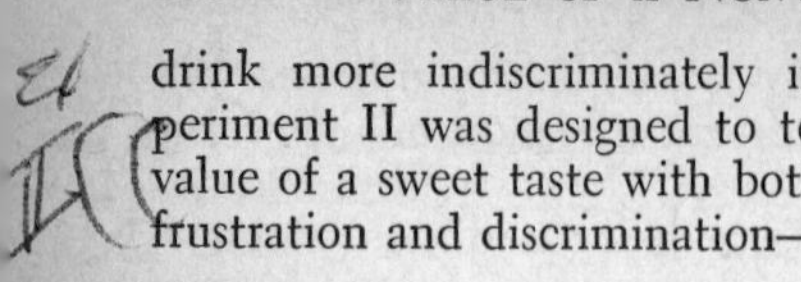

drink more indiscriminately if neither was sweet. Experiment II was designed to test further the reinforcing value of a sweet taste with both of these latter factors—frustration and discrimination—eliminated.

Method

The laboratory was normally kept dimly lighted by a shielded 25-watt lamp. At 9:00 A.M., 11:00 A.M., 1:00 P.M., 3:00 P.M., and 5:00 P.M., the experimenter entered the room, turned on a bright overhead light and inserted the saccharine bottle, always on the same side for a given animal. A bottle of plain water was always present on the opposite side. The subjects were the same ones which had been used in Experiment I, the hunger regime was the same, and the saccharine solution was of the same concentration (1.30 grams per liter) and on the same side as in Experiment I. On each trial the saccharine bottle was left in position for exactly 10 minutes and the measure of instrumental behavior was the amount of the solution consumed. It was expected that if a sweet taste was reinforcing then the turning on of the light, the presence of the experimenter, the sound of the bottle being inserted, and the visual presence of the bottle would be a cue-pattern to which approach and drinking would become conditioned. The ten-minute trials were continued for 18 days—a total of 90 trials.

Results

Acquisition of instrumental drinking in response to the environmental cue-pattern appeared to continue throughout the 18-day period for hungry animals, although approaching an asymptote toward the end of training. Satiated animals on the other hand showed no signs of acquisition. The results are depicted in figure 1, which shows the average ccs. per 10-minute trial per rat. The results are smoothed in the figure by using successive sets of three days' trials (15 trials per rat for each point on the curve).

It is apparent in figure 1 that the satiated rats show no increase in propensity to drink saccharine whereas hungry animals show progressive acquisition. The acquisition in hungry animals is well beyond the one per cent level of confidence (t, for first point versus last point, = 4.9, df. = 5). Thus when the frustration and discrimination possible in Experiment I are eliminated a conventional acquisition curve is obtained. This argues against extinction of an acquired reward as an explanation of the failure to get progressive acquisition in Experiment I.

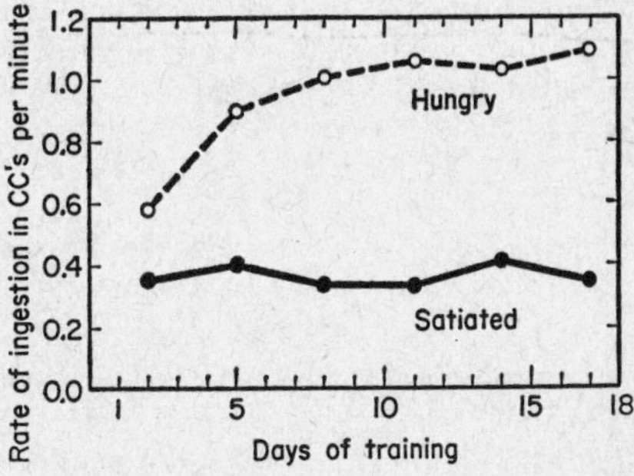

Fig. 1. Acquisition of Drinking of the Saccharine Solution (1.30 grams per liter) in Response to a Specific Cue-Pattern Accompanying Availability of the Solution.

It should be borne in mind that the same animals were used in both experiments. Thus a sweet taste was shown to retain its reinforcing value for hungry animals over a lengthy period in which it could have extinguished if it were an acquired reward. Also the rate of ingestion for hungry animals was much higher by the end of Experiment II than it was even on the first day of Experiment I. Over the first day of Experiment I the hungry animals drank at a rate of 0.17 ccs. per minute, whereas the last point on the curve for hungry animals in figure 1 represents a rate of 1.09 ccs. per minute.[2] This difference is

[2] A methodological point worth mentioning is that the hungry animals consistently drank the least at the 1:00 P.M. test, which came just before their daily feeding—at a time when they were presumably most hungry. This runs counter to the overall relation between hunger and saccharine drinking and is interpreted by the writers as due to the conflicting habit of loitering at the front of the cage where food was soon to be introduced.

complicated by the fact that in Experiment I the animals were asleep part of the time but it probably reflects in addition the fact that the unlimited drinking periods of Experiment I allowed any painful effects of too full a stomach to motivate avoidance of drinking behavior. The difference is in a direction opposed to the hypothesis that a sweet taste is an acquired reward which extinguishes with performance of the instrumental response. The reinforcing effect was still going strong after 10 days of unlimited drinking in Experiment I and 18 days with five 10-minute drinking periods per day in Experiment II.

EXPERIMENT III

Purpose

The main purpose of Experiment III was to test the reinforcing value of a sweet taste in a more conventional animal-learning situation than that used in Experiments I and II. A second purpose was to continue the same animals in a further learning task to give further opportunity for the reward value of a sweet taste to extinguish if it is an acquired reward. A third purpose was to get a rough idea of the order of magnitude of the reinforcing values of saccharine and food with hungry animals.

Method

The same hungry animals used in Experiments I and II served as subjects in Experiment III. Of the six hungry rats used in the first two experiments, one died of whirling disease between experiments, so only five animals were available for Experiment III. The learning task was acquisition of a position habit in a standard T-maze. The stem and each arm of the maze were 21 inches long and four and one-half inches wide. The interior of the stem was painted grey, that of one arm was painted white and that of the other black. The ends of each goal box were made of wire screening to provide cues very similar to those in the animal's previous experience with drinking from the saccharine bottle in its wire-screen living cage. A Springfield timer recorded running time via a microswitch which started the timer when the door of the starting box was opened and another microswitch which stopped the clock when the animal's weight landed on a hinged floor at the far end of the arm. Retracing was prevented by dropping a door as soon as the animal entered a particular arm. The correct side for a given animal always had a bottle of saccharine solution (1.30 grams per liter); the incorrect side had a bottle of plain water. Throughout Experiment III the animals had a supply of water from a water tray in their living cages—thus they were satiated for thirst, and the only time they drank from a glass tube during the experiment was in the maze. All trials were run in the evening, starting about 8:00 P.M.; the daily feeding of 8 grams (dry weight) of Purina flour mixed with water was given at noon. The procedure was as follows:

1. Four forced runs, two to the saccharine side and two to the water side. The forced runs were spaced over two days, one of each kind per day, balanced for order. On each trial the rat was confined in the end box for eight minutes.
2. Forty-two free-choice trials, three per day for 14 days, the trials on a given day being spaced about one half-hour apart. On each trial the rat was confined in the end box for four minutes.

Results

All animals showed prompt acquisition in terms of both time and errors. The results are summarized in the three curves shown in figure 2. Curve A shows acquisition in terms of frequency of correct choice; the frequency scores plotted use per cent of correct choices on each day's set of three trials for the five animals. Thus the N at each point in the curve is 15 animal-trials. Curve B shows acquisition in terms of time to reach the end of the arm on correct choices. Every animal made at least one correct choice per day, and the value plotted in the curve is the median, over the five animals, of each animal's median daily performance. Curve C shows the mean rate of consumption of saccharine solution. The daily rate per minute was determined for each animal and these values were averaged over the five animals to get the points plotted.

An important relationship was found between rate

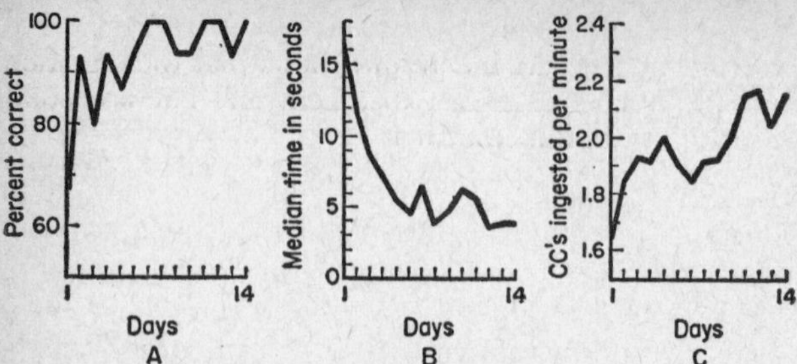

Fig. 2. Acquisition in a T-Maze with Saccharine Solution (1.30 grams per liter) as Reward: (A) Frequency of Correct Choices, (B) Time to Reach Correct Side, (C) Rate of Ingestion of Solution in the Goal Box.

of ingestion of saccharine solution and maze performance. Animals whose rate of drinking tended to be low during the four minutes of confinement in the goal box also tended to be poor learners both in terms of time scores and frequency scores. In other words if they did not drink the saccharine avidly they also did not perform well in getting to the solution. The relationship is depicted in figure 3.

Another interesting finding was that the average rate of consumption was much greater in Experiment III than in either of the preceding experiments. It has already been noted that the rate of ingestion was much greater

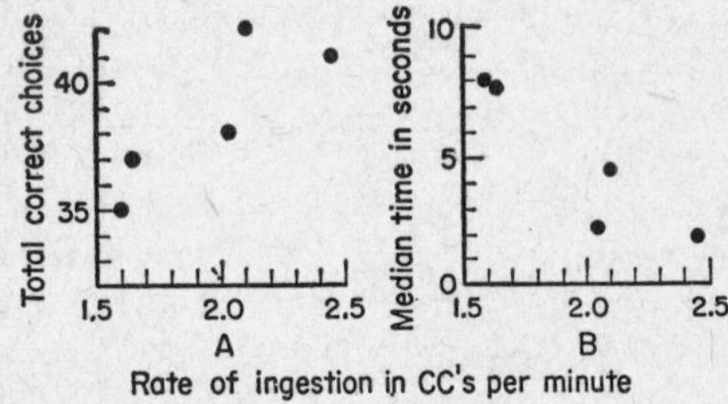

Fig. 3. Relation Between Mean Amount of Saccharine Drinking in the Four Minute Confinement and (A) Frequency of Correct Choice on All Trials and (B) Median Running Time During the Last Half of Training.

in Experiment II than in Experiment I and a comparison of figure 1 and figure 2-C readily shows that the ingestion rate was much greater in Experiment III. The last point on the curve in Experiment II showed a rate of 1.09 ccs. per minute whereas the last day in Experiment III was 2.16 ccs. per minute. This result probably can be attributed to the greater specificity of the cues in the maze situation and to the fact that only four minutes of drinking were allowed at a time, thus minimizing the chance of filling up and avoiding the bottle. However, this result, like the rest of the findings in Experiment III, argues against extinction of the reward value of the non-nourishing sweet taste.

Moreover, the motivating power of the sweet taste was quite impressive. The two fastest animals appeared to run at top speed and were consistently close to two seconds at the end of training. The final median time of 3.8 seconds is slower than that obtained in the same apparatus by other rats rewarded with food, who achieved a median of about two seconds. However, the time is still of a low enough order of magnitude to indicate considerable reinforcement value of a sweet taste for hungry animals.

DISCUSSION

The experiments prove that a non-nourishing but sweet-tasting substance served as a reinforcement for instrumental learning. Hunger was presumably in no way reduced by the saccharine solution, yet hungry animals clearly demonstrated acquisition in the three different learning situations in which the reward was a saccharine solution.

The possibility that the sweet taste was an acquired reward seems very unlikely—on two counts. For one thing, previously experienced sweet tastes (e.g., rat's milk, conversion of starch to sugar in the mouth, etc.) are very unlikely to have been as sweet as the concentrated saccharine solution used. Thus the sweet taste used would be at an unfavorable point on the generalization gradient as an acquired reward stimulus if we make the usual assumption that the generalization gradient falls in either direction from the stimulus intensity reinforced. Moreover, the sweet taste did not lose its reward value throughout the three experiments, with the ingestion of thousands of ccs. of saccharine solution and no doubt millions of instrumental tongue movements. Since the visual, kinesthetic, tactile, and gustatory pattern accompanying this ingestion in all three experiments (drinking from a glass tube protruding from a visible graduated cylinder through quarter-inch wire mesh) received no primary reinforcement, it would be expected that any *acquired* reward value of a sweet taste would have extinguished for this pattern.

The findings are thus at variance with the molar principle of reinforcement used by Hull (4), which identifies primary reinforcement with "need reduction." Hull admittedly chose need reduction on the grounds that from a Darwinian point of view reduction of a survival need is very likely to be accompanied by a "reinforcing state of affairs," and at the molar level this principle may be predictive in a high proportion of instances of instrumental learning. However, it does not designate the *mechanism* by which natural selection has managed to make need-reducing events reinforcing, and it is unable to predict the present results in which reinforcement is obtained in the absence of need reduction. The findings highlight the desirability of a theory concerning the mechanism (or mechanisms) by which natural selection has achieved adaptive instrumental learning.

At a more molecular level, Miller and Dollard (5) have proposed *reduction of drive* as the occasion for a reinforcing state of affairs and they tentatively identify drive with intensity of stimulation. The present findings are at variance with their position in that hunger drive, in the usual sense of the concept, is not at all reduced by the saccharine solution. Thus, as mentioned earlier, saccharine is allegedly excreted without chemical change and its ingestion has no effect on food intake (3). However, it may be postulated that part of the total stimulation in the case of hunger consists of proprioceptive return from the striped-muscle tension occasioned by the hunger state. It may further be postulated that a sweet taste relaxes the striped muscles—at the very least the animal stands still while ingesting the solution—and this innate relaxation would provide stimulus reduction and consequent acquisition of instrumental responses. Thus a closer analysis of the physiological effects of a sweet taste may show that the present results are consistent with Miller and Dollard's position.

While the experiments were aimed mainly at providing evidence relevant to the need-reduction and drive-reduction theories, a brief comment should be made on the relation of the results to other positions on the reinforcement process. The results in no way conflict with or provide support for the relatively empirical and circular systems of Skinner (7), Thorndike (8), and Tolman (9). The results merely demonstrate that with hungry animals a saccharine solution is a "reinforcing stimulus" in Skinner's terms, is a "reward" or "satisfier" in Thorndike's terms, and probably is "demanded" in Tolman's terms. The results are also consistent with Guthrie's (2) more theoretical and less circular position involving the mechanism of stimulus change and protection of the last response from relearning. In Guthrie's terms the results demonstrate that ingesting the sweet substance innately produces a stimulus change which can be observed to be very much the same as that produced by presenting food to the hungry animal (i.e., cessation of exploration, maintained ingestion, and so forth) and it is therefore not surprising that the change is big enough to protect the instrumental response. Another theory which cannot escape mention in the present context is the unpopular "beneceptor" theory of Troland (10), which holds that the reinforcing value of a reward lies in the quality of the stimulation produced by the reward. The findings are a natural fit to his theory—which argues that stimulation of receptors for sweet is all that is needed to strengthen an instrumental act.

In conclusion the question should be answered as to whether any novel hypotheses concerning the reinforcement process are indicated by the results. The chief suggestion the authors have to make is that stimulation and performance of a consummatory response appears to be more important to instrumental learning—in a primary, not acquired, way—than the drive satisfaction which the consummatory response normally achieves. The present experiments were essentially sham-feeding experiments in which the animal was innately stimulated to ingest a substance which did not change his state of hunger, and the result was acquisition, without extinction, of the instrumental responses. Thus it would appear that *eliciting* the consummatory response of ingestion was the critical factor. This suggestion is in line with Wolfe and Kaplon's (11) finding that with total food intake held constant, the reward value of eating is a function of amount of consummatory activity required to ingest the food.

SUMMARY

1. A non-nourishing but sweet-tasting substance was shown in three successive learning situations to be an effective reward for instrumental learning, its reward value depending on the state of hunger present.

2. The possibility that the sweet taste was an acquired reward rather than a primary reward was shown to be extremely unlikely.

3. The findings demonstrate the expected limitations of Hull's molar "need reduction" theory of reinforcement and the necessity of exploring indirect reduction of striped-muscle tension as a drive-reduction factor in Miller and Dollard's theory of reinforcement. The results are consistent with Guthrie's last-response theory of reinforcement, and demonstrate that a sweet taste is "reinforcing" in Skinner's system, "satisfying" in Thorndike's system, and "demanded" in Tolman's system.

4. It is suggested that elicitation of the consummatory response appears to be a more critical *primary* reinforcing factor in instrumental learning than the drive reduction subsequently achieved.

REFERENCES

1. BEEBE-CENTER, J. G., BLACK, P., HOFFMAN, A. C., AND WADE, MARJORIE: Relative per diem consumption as a measure of preference in the rat. *J. comp. physiol. Psychol.* 1948, **41**, 239-251.

2. GUTHRIE, E. R.: *The psychology of learning.* New York: Harper, 1935.
3. HAUSMANN, M. F.: The behavior of rats in choosing food. II Differentiation between sugar and saccharine. *J. comp. Psychol.* 1933, **15,** 419-428.
4. HULL, C. L.: *Principles of behavior.* New York: Appleton-Century, 1943.
5. MILLER, N. E. AND DOLLARD, J.: *Social learning and imitation.* New Haven: Yale Press, 1941.
6. RICHTER, C. P. AND CAMPBELL, KATHRYNE.: Taste thresholds and taste preferences of rats for five common sugars. *J. Nutrition.* 1940, **20,** 31-46.
7. SKINNER, B. F.: *The behavior of organisms.* New York: Appleton-Century, 1938.
8. THORNDIKE, E. L.: *Animal intelligence.* New York: Macmillan, 1911.
9. TOLMAN, E. C.: *Purposive behavior in animals and men.* New York: Appleton-Century, 1932.
10. TROLAND, L. T.: *The fundamentals of human motivation.* New York: Van Nostrand, 1928.
11. WOLFE, J. B. AND KAPLON, M. D.: Effect of amount of reward and consummative activity on learning in chickens. *J. comp. Psychol.* 1941, **31,** 353-361.

10

Reward Effects of Food Via Stomach Fistula Compared with Those of Food Via Mouth[1]

NEAL E. MILLER AND MARION L. KESSEN

Yale University

Motivation and reward are closely related. For example, if an animal is not motivated by the drive of hunger, food is not an effective reward. Furthermore, the food that rewards the hungry animal so that it learns, also tends to reduce the strength of its hunger drive so that it eventually becomes satiated. These functional relationships have led to the drive-reduction hypothesis of reinforcement which states that a prompt reduction in the strength of a drive has the effect of rewarding immediately preceding responses (2, 6, 7). According to this hypothesis the rewarding effects of food are due to the fact that it reduces the strength of the hunger drive, and the relative ineffectiveness of food as a reward after the animal has become satiated is due to the fact that little if any drive is present to be reduced.

The present experiment is one of a series designed to analyze the mechanism of satiation and its relationship to the rewarding effects of food. The first two experiments in this series compared the hunger-reducing effects of food via stomach fistula with those of food via mouth. The measure of hunger in the first of these, Kohn (4), was the rate of performance of an instrumental response

This article originally appeared in the *Journal of Comparative and Physiological Psychology*, 45, 1952, pp. 555-563.

[1] This study was supported by funds from the Institute of Human Relations. A preliminary report of it was given as part of a paper read at the 1951 meetings of the APA (8).

(panel-pushing) periodically reinforced by food; in the second, Berkun, Kessen, and Miller (1), it was a consummatory response (amount of milk drunk). Both measures showed exactly the same pattern of results: (*a*) 14 cc. of isotonic saline injected by fistula directly into the stomach of hungry albino rats produced relatively little effect, (*b*) a similar volume of enriched milk injected directly into the stomach produced a prompt reduction in the rate of performance of the instrumental response and the amount of the consummatory response, and (*c*) the same volume of enriched milk taken normally by mouth produced an even greater reduction in the responses. From these results it seems reasonable to conclude that milk injected directly into the stomach produces a prompt reduction in the strength of hunger and that milk taken normally by mouth produces an even greater reduction.

If milk injected directly into the stomach produces a prompt reduction in the strength of hunger, the drive-reduction hypothesis of reinforcement demands that it should act as a reward to produce the learning of new responses. That food injected directly into the stomach may indeed serve as a reward is suggested by the results which Hull *et al.* (3) secured in an exploratory experiment on a dog with an esophageal fistula. Unfortunately, the original data of this experiment were lost, but the authors' notes indicate that the animal learned to choose the side of a simple maze where it received food through the esophageal fistula in preference to the side where a catheter was inserted but no food injected.

The main purpose of the present experiment was to determine whether food injected via fistula directly into the stomach of hungry albino rats would serve as a reward to reinforce the learning of a simple habit. The essential procedure involved giving hungry rats with small plastic fistulas sewn into their stomachs injections of enriched milk when they made the correct choice on a T maze and an injection of isotonic saline when they made an incorrect choice. Learning the correct choice would demonstrate the reward value of an injection of food; it would also serve as a control to rule out the possibility that the reductions in instrumental and in consummatory responses observed in the first two experiments were caused by nausea motivating conflicting responses rather than by a genuine reduction in the strength of the hunger drive. Finally, such learning would not be expected from the hypothesis, recently advanced by Sheffield (9, 10, 11), that the critical factor in reinforcement is the elicitation of a prepotent consummatory response.

A second purpose of the experiment was to compare the rewarding effects of food injected directly into the stomach with those of food taken normally by mouth. This was accomplished by training a second group of animals that received a dish of milk when they went to the correct side of the T maze and a dish of isotonic saline when they went to the incorrect side. From the fact that food by mouth produces a greater reduction in the strength of hunger than food via fistula, the drive-reduction hypothesis predicts that it should serve as a stronger reward and hence produce faster learning. A similar prediction would also be made from the fact that one would expect the cues involved in oral ingestion to have learned reward value.

Since it might be argued that the effect of reward begins with the first sip, when milk is taken by mouth, but only after a considerable volume of milk has been injected directly into the stomach, a third group was run exactly like the second one except that the presentation of the dishes of milk or saline was delayed 7 min. and 35 sec., the time required to complete an injection.

PROCEDURE

The subjects in this experiment were 17 male, albino rats of Sprague-Dawley strain approximately 150 days old at the start of the experiment. All of them had small plastic fistulas sewn into their stomachs, threaded between the skin and the body wall and projecting approximately ½ in. from the back of the neck. These fistulas were inserted according to the procedure described by Kohn (4).

The apparatus is illustrated in Figure 1. It consisted of a T maze. The starting compartment was painted black; it had a slotted lid through which a small rubber tube descended to the animal's fistula, and a false back which could be pushed forward when it was necessary to force recalcitrant subjects to make a choice. The two arms of the maze, which also served as the goal boxes, were made quite distinctive (*a*) so that it would be easy for the cues in the correct one to acquire learned reward value to help compensate for any delay in the effects of the injection, and (*b*) to minimize the generalization of this learned reward value to the cues in the incorrect goal box (12). The goal box to the left (in the diagram) was painted gray and had a floor consisting of ½-in.-guage wire mesh which was bisected longitudinally by an aluminum covered wooden strip ⅞ in. high and ¾ wide. The goal box to the right was painted with vertical black and white stripes 1 in. wide and had a window-screen floor.

In order to allow a ½-in. opening at the top through which the small rubber tube could descend to the fistula, but to discourage the rats from trying to jump up and poke their heads through this opening, the sides of the two goal boxes slanted inward at a 12° angle toward the top. The front of each goal box was a hinged door through which the animals could be removed. In order to allow the experimenter to observe the animals in the goal boxes, the top 7¼ in. of this hinged front side was made of transparent plastic.

Lowering the door at the front of the starting compartment automatically started an electric clock. When it put one of its front feet across a little break in the metal mesh in the floor 4 in. from the entrance of either goal box, the animal completed a circuit allowing a subthreshold current to actuate an electronic relay which stopped the clock. Then the experimenter closed the door behind it so that the animal was confined in the goal box. The experimenter operated the doors by foot pedals.

A small rubber tube ran from the rat's fistula up through the top of the maze over a pulley on the far side of which a light counterweight picked up the slack. Beyond the counterweight the tube was attached to an ordinary hypodermic syringe containing the liquid to be injected.

At the end of each goal box was a small hinged door through which dishes of milk or saline could be inserted.

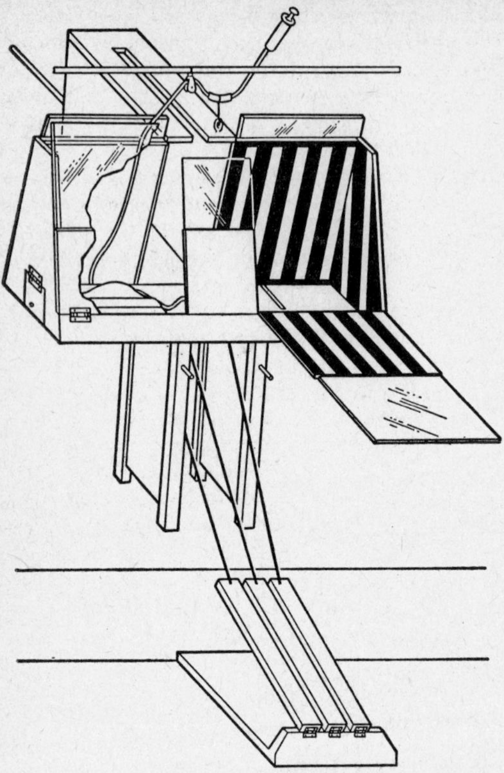

Fig. 1. The T maze

The starting box has a false back which can be pushed forward by a rod projecting through the back. The starting box and each of the goal boxes have doors sliding up from below, which are operated by foot pedals. Opening the door to the starting box closes a microswitch and starts a clock which is stopped when the animal steps across the small gap in the floor of either goal box and operates an electronic relay. The top 7½ in. of the front of the apparatus is transparent plastic to allow the experimenter to observe the animal. In the diagram the hinged front of the right goal box is opened; a portion of the left one is cut so that an animal can be seen being injected with milk via fistula. Hinged doors at the end of each goal box allow dishes of milk or saline to be inserted.

In order to speed up the procedure and to rule out any possibility that drops of spilled milk or the odor of milk could serve as a reward for the injected animals, two pieces of apparatus were used, one for the animals receiving injections via fistula and another for those receiving milk by dish. These T mazes were identical except for the fact that in the first one the striped compartment was on the right and in the second it was on the left. It had originally been planned to reverse the roles of these two pieces of apparatus in the second replication of the experiment as a control on the improbable possibility that differences between them influenced learning. Inasmuch as the results of the first replication were statistically reliable, however, no second one was run.

The diet used in this experiment consisted of milk enriched with cream, starch, casein, vitamins, and minerals according to the formula described in previous articles (1, 4). This supplied 2.1 calories per cc. It was supplemented by a mash of 50 per cent ground Purina Laboratory Chow and 50 per cent water in amounts sufficient to bring the animal's total daily intake to 50 calories.

Habituation. Postoperative care of the animals was similar to that described by Kohn (4). To avoid possible distress (suggested by exploratory work), the experimental animals were first habituated to progressively increasing injections of milk. Each animal was injected with milk twice a day at 11 A.M. and 3 P.M. The first injection was 2 cc. and on each subsequent injection the amount was increased 2 cc. until 12 cc. had been injected. Enough wet mash was given at approximately 4:30 P.M. to bring the total intake to 50 cal. Injections were given on a small perch at the rate the animals normally drank, 1 cc. every 35 sec. The animals to be fed by mouth were habituated in exactly the same way except that they received progressively increasing amounts of milk in dishes in their home cages.

Training. Before habituation the animals were randomly divided into three groups:

1. *Stomach injection* animals received an injection of 14 cc. of enriched milk via fistula when they went to the correct side and 14 cc. of isotonic saline when to the incorrect. For two animals the correct (milk) side was

to the right; for three it was to the left. (Seven operated animals were originally prepared for these groups. One, however, was discarded before the first trial because its fistula leaked, and the second had to have a new fistula put in after five training trials, and then died following an operation for a tumor after 26 days of training during which it showed definite signs of learning.) Before being placed in the starting box, the animals had a small rubber tube slipped over their fistula and firmly tied with a thread. In order to avoid injecting air into the animal, this tube was collapsed by gentle suction from a hypodermic syringe after which the free end was sealed off by a little spring clip. As soon as the animal stopped the clock, the door was closed behind it, the syringe containing the proper substance was connected to the tube, the clip was removed, and the first 1 cc. (plus an extra 3.15 cc. required to fill the rubber tube and the plastic fistula) was injected. Thereafter 1 cc. was injected every 35 sec. so that the average rate of injection approximated the rate at which animals had been found to drink normally by mouth. The injection lasted for 7 min. 35 sec.; the animals were allowed to remain in the compartment 3 min. longer and then were removed to their home cages. Approximately 15 min. before the first run each day, while the animals were being weighed, they received an injection of 1 cc. water to clear the fistula and, if the last injection of the day had been milk, another 1 cc. of water was injected before they received their supplementary diet of wet mash.

2. *Mouth, No delay* animals received dishes containing 14 cc. of milk or saline in the correct or incorrect goal boxes, respectively. These dishes were inserted through the hinged door at the end of the sections at the same time that the injections of animals in the preceding group were begun. For three rats the correct side was to the right, and for the other three to the left. The animals in this group remained in the goal boxes the same length of time as those in the first group.

3. *Mouth, Delay* animals received their dishes of 14 cc. of milk for a correct choice or saline for an incorrect one after a delay of 7 min. 35 sec., the time that it normally took to complete an injection. After this delay

these animals were left in the goal box with the dish of milk or saline for another period of approximately 7 min. 35 sec. For three of these animals the correct side was to the right, for three to the left.

At approximately 10 A.M. each animal in each of the three groups was given a trial during which it was free to choose either side. As soon as it stepped over the break in the floor of a goal box and stopped the clock, the door was closed behind it and the substance, milk for a correct choice or saline for an incorrect one, was administered. Approximately 4 hr. later, each animal was given a second trial during which the door to the previously chosen side was closed so that it was forced to turn in the opposite direction and receive the other kind of substance. If an animal failed to run within 3 min. on any trial, the false back of the starting box was gradually pushed forward, forcing the animal to the choice point; if it failed to choose within 7 additional minutes, the false back was pushed all of the way forward so that the animal was forced out of the choice point into a goal box. Approximately an hour after the forced trial the animals were given enough wet mash in their home cages to bring their daily intake to a total of 50 calories.

Training of the stomach-injection animals was continued for 40 days. Because the other two groups had already learned, their training was discontinued after 25 days.

In some animals there developed an infection along the side of the fistula. Cultures showed that the infections continued a typical intestinal bacteria, *Escherichia coli*, which presumably seeped through the incision where the fistula was sewn into the stomach. Such infections were treated by making a pinpoint incision at the place of infection, draining it and sprinkling powdered sulfathiazole on this area. As a preventive measure the animals were given powdered aureomycin three or four times a week in their diet of wet mash.

RESULTS

Figure 2 shows the percentage of correct choices (to the milk side) made by the animals in the three groups on the morning trials which were free choice. It can be seen that all three groups learned. In order to test the reliability of improvement for the animals which received injections directly into the stomach, the number of correct choices made by each animal on the first 15 free-choice trials was compared with that on the last 15. Chi-square tests, corrected for discontinuity, showed that the improvement was statistically reliable for each one of the five animals in that group. For the individual animals the probability of securing the observed differences

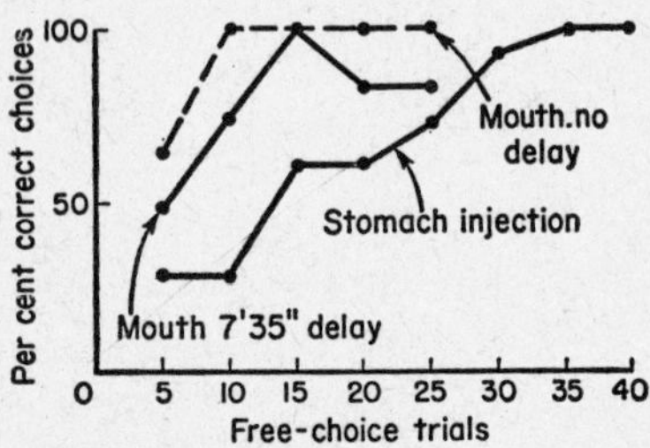

Fig. 2. Percentage of choices to the correct (milk) side on free-choice trials

After making five successive correct choices on the eleventh to fifteenth trials, one animal in the Mouth, Delay Group reverted to a consistent position habit on the incorrect side. This one animal contributed all the errors made by this group after the first ten trials.

in the predicted direction by chance are: .05, .05, .01, .001, and .001. Furthermore, the three animals tested in the preliminary experiment using a slightly different apparatus (8) also learned to go consistently ($p = .02$, .01, and .001) to the side (two right and one left) on which milk was injected via fistula.

Comparing the different groups shows that milk taken immediately by mouth produced the fastest learning, milk taken by mouth after a delay produced the next fastest learning, and milk injected directly into the stomach produced the slowest learning. In order to test the reliability of these differences each animal was given a score which was the number of correct choices during the first 25 free-choice trials. Then *t* tests were made. These are summarized in Table 1. It can be seen that the superiority of the animals fed milk by mouth (either immediately or after a delay) over those who received it via fistula is statistically reliable.

Figure 3 shows the mean running speed to milk of the animals in the three groups. When the free choice in the morning was correct, this was the running speed

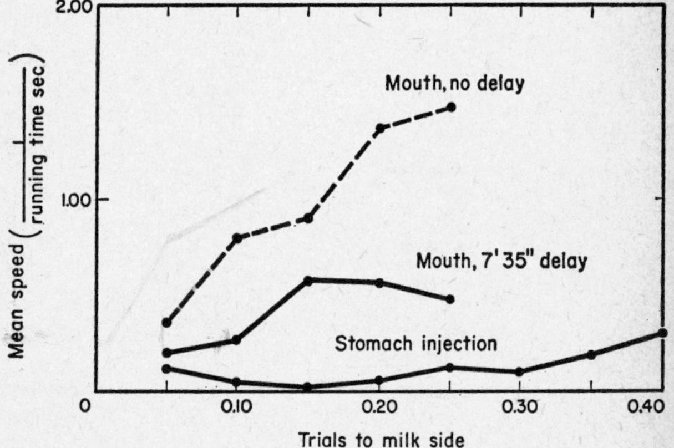

Fig. 3. Speed of running to the compartment in which milk was given.

on that trial; when it was incorrect, this was the running speed on the afternoon forced trial to the milk side. It can be seen that the differences among the speed scores of the three groups are exactly the same as those among the error scores. In order to test the reliability of these differences, the time scores of each animal on each trial were converted to logs. This conversion was made to normalize the distribution. Then each animal was given a score consisting of the sum of the log times on the first 25 trials, and *t* tests were made for the differences among the means of the three groups. These are summarized in

TABLE 1

Reliabilities of the differences between the groups on days 1 to 25

Group	Errors in free-choice	Log time to milk side
Stomach Injection vs. Mouth, No Delay	.001*	.001
Stomach Injection vs. Mouth, Delay	.038	.001
Mouth, Delay vs. Mouth, No Delay	.070	.003

* Probability of getting by chance as large a difference in the predicted direction.

Table 1, which shows that all the differences are highly reliable.

Further evidence that the injection of milk directly into the stomach produced learning whereas that of

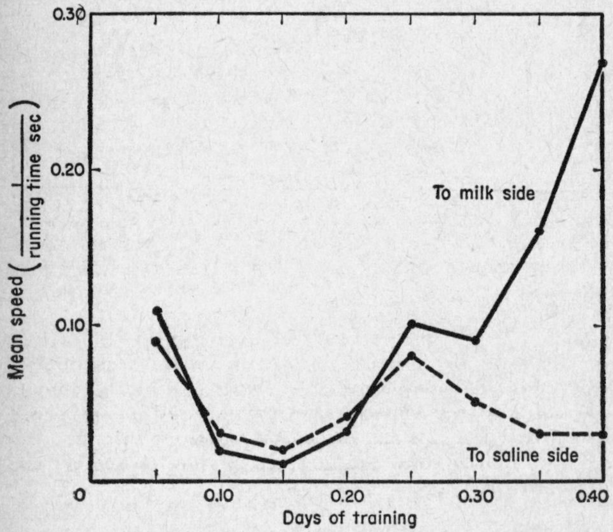

*Fig. 4. Speed of run to milk versus speed of run to isotonic saline for animals receiving injections via fistula.**

* *The curve represented by the solid line in this figure is the same as the bottom curve in Fig. 3 except that the scale has been considerably magnified.*

saline did not, is presented in Figure 4. This figure presents the speed of running to the compartment in which milk was injected compared with that to the compartment in which saline was injected. At the beginning of training there was no difference between these two speeds. During the first 15 trials the speed of running to both compartments decreased. It seems probable that this decrease was produced by the extinction of initial exploratory tendencies, but it may have been due to a slight discomfort produced by the injections during the early part of training and gradually adapting out or becoming counteracted by the reward effects.[2] From the fifteenth trial on there is a progressive increase in the speed of running to the compartment where milk was injected while the speed to the compartment where saline was injected remains at approximately the same low level. The difference in the speeds of running to the milk and

[2] That such discomfort can be produced is suggested by the results of a fourth group of five animals which were run as a part of the original design of this experiment but relegated to this footnote because the behavior and results suggested an artifact from discomfort produced by the injection. These animals were run under exactly the same conditions as the first group except that during habituation and training their injection was given almost ten times faster so that 14 cc. required between 45 sec. and 1 min. During the last 15 free-choice trials, chi-square tests showed that three of these animals were consistently going to the saline side ($p = .01$, .001, .001) and two to the milk side ($p = .01$ and .001). Because the avoidance of the milk side showed up so early in training, none of the differences between the first and last 15 free-choice trials is reliable for the animals preferring saline, but for the animals choosing milk these differences are reliable at .04 and .001 levels, respectively. The fact that the animals preferring the saline side had to be forced (their average speed to saline on the last five trials was somewhat slower than that of the animals injected at the normal rate, but their average speed to milk was much slower) suggests that they were avoiding milk rather than approaching saline. Because milk curdles and leaves the stomach much more slowly than saline, it seems reasonable to assume that the fast injection of large amounts of milk would be more likely to produce distress than similar injections of isotonic saline.

saline compartments (as calculated by t tests for the sum of the log times on the last 5 trials to each) would be expected in the predicted direcion by chance less than 1 time in 100. It is another indication of the reward effect of injecting milk directly into the stomach.

DISCUSSION

The results show (*a*) that milk injected directly into the stomach can serve as a reward to produce learning, and (*b*) that milk taken normally by mouth serves as a stronger reward to produce faster learning. Both results are exactly what was predicted from the drive-reduction hypothesis and the evidence (1, 4) that milk by fistula produces a prompt reduction in the strength of hunger while milk by mouth produces an even greater reduction. The reward effect of milk injected directly into the stomach would not readily be predicted from Sheffield's (9, 10, 11) hypothesis that reinforcement is critically related to the ability of the goal object to elicit a dependable, prepotent response when presented.

The faster learning of the animals which received milk by mouth would be expected from the fact that this procedure produces a greater reduction in the strength of the drive. It would also be predicted from the fact that one would expect the cues involved in oral ingestion to have learned reward value, but if one holds to a strict drive-reduction hypothesis of learned rewards, this reduces to the same factor of drive-reduction (5, 6, 7). It is also quite possible that the reduction in the strength of drive is not quite as prompt when food is injected into the stomach as when it is taken by mouth.

Finally, the fact that the injected animals learned to choose the milk side serves as a control to rule out the possibility that the effects of the injection of milk into the stomach in the preceding experiments (1, 4) were only the production of nausea rather than a reduction in the strength of the hunger drive.

SUMMARY

1. Seventeen male, albino rats had small plastic fistulas sewn into their stomachs. Then they were given training trials during which they received enriched milk when they went to the correct side of a simple T maze and isotonic saline when they went to the incorrect side. They were divided into three groups trained respectively under the following conditions:

a. The substances, 14 cc. of milk for a correct or saline for an incorrect choice, were injected directly into the stomach at the rate at which the animals normally drank.

b. Dishes containing 14 cc. of milk for a correct or saline for an an incorrect choice were inserted into the end of the goal box immediately after the animal had made its choice.

c. Dishes containing 14 cc. of milk or saline were inserted into the end of the goal box after a delay of 7 min. 35 sec., the time required to complete an injection for the animals in *a.*

2. All animals were given two trials a day motivated by hunger. On the first trial the animal was free to go in either direction; this trial was used to measure correct choices. On the second trial, given 4 hr. later, the animal was forced to go in the opposite direction and receive the other substance.

3. The animals which received injections directly into their stomachs learned to choose the milk side within 40 days of training. Both the decrease in errors and the faster speed to the milk side were statistically highly reliable.

4. The animals which received milk by mouth, either immediately or after a delay, learned faster than those which received milk via fistula. The differences in both the speed and error scores were statistically reliable.

5. These results show that milk injected directly into the stomach serves as a reward to produce learning, but that milk taken normally by mouth serves as a stronger reward to produce faster learning. The results confirm the prediction from the drive-reduction hypothesis of reinforcement and fail to confirm the prediction from the

prepotent consummatory response hypothesis of reinforcement. They serve as a control to show that the decrements in instrumental and consummatory responses observed in preceding experiments were produced by reductions in hunger rather than by nausea.

REFERENCES

1. BERKUN, M. M., KESSEN, M. L., & MILLER, N. E. Hunger-reducing effects of food by stomach fistula versus food by mouth measured by a consummatory response. *J. comp. physiol. Psychol.*, 1952, **45**, 550-554.
2. HULL, C. L. *Principles of behavior*. New York: D. Appleton-Century, 1943.
3. HULL, C. L., LIVINGSTON, J. R., ROUSE, R. O., & BARKER, A. N. True, sham, and esophageal feeding as reinforcements. *J. comp. physiol. Psychol.*, 1951, **44**, 236-245.
4. KOHN, M. Satiation of hunger from stomach versus mouth feeding. *J. comp. physiol. Psychol.*, 1951, **44**, 412-422.
5. MILLER, N. E. Learnable drives and rewards. In S. Stevens (Ed.), *Handbook of experimental psychology*. New York: Wiley, 1951.
6. MILLER, N. E. Comments on multiple-process conceptions of learning. *Psychol. Rev.*, 1951, **58**, 357-363.
7. MILLER, N. E., & DOLLARD, J. *Social learning and imitation*. New Haven, Conn.: Yale Univer. Press, 1941.
8. MILLER, N. E., KESSEN, M. L., & KOHN, M. The drive-reducing and reinforcing effects of food injected via fistula into the stomach. *Amer. Psychologist*, 1951, **6**, 280-281. (Abstract)
9. SHEFFIELD, F. D., & ROBY, T. B. Reward value of a non-nutritive sweet taste. *J. comp. physiol. Psychol.*, 1950, **43**, 471-481.
10. SHEFFIELD, F. D., WULFF, J. J., & BACKER, R. Reward value of copulation without sex drive reduction. *J. comp. physiol. Psychol.*, 1951, **44**, 3-8.

11. SHEFFIELD, F. D. The contiguity principle in learning theory. *Psychol. Rev.*, 1951, **58**, 362-367.
12. SPENCE, K. W. The role of secondary reinforcement in delayed reward learning. *Psychol. Rev.*, 1947, **54**, 1-8.

11

Discrimination Learning by Rhesus Monkeys to Visual-Exploration Motivation[1]

ROBERT A. BUTLER
University of Wisconsin

Experiments conducted at the University of Wisconsin Primate Laboratory have demonstrated that rhesus monkeys learn the solution of mechanical puzzles to no other incentive than that provided by the manipulation of the puzzle devices (4, 1, 2) and that these manipulatory responses will persist during prolonged repetitive testing (3). Recently, monkeys have been trained without food or other special incentives to discriminate between differentially colored sets of screw eyes (5). A manipulation drive has been postulated as the motivational basis for this type of behavior, and Harlow postulates that manipulation drive is "one of a class of externally elicited drives" (3, p. 293).

The present experiments were designed to test the efficacy of another kind of externally elicited motive, that of visual exploration. Monkeys both in their home cages and in test situations continually follow movements of objects and people in their field of vision and persistently explore their environment visually.

Two preliminary experiments were conducted to inves-

This article originally appeared in the *Journal of Comparative and Physiological Psychology*, 46, 1953, pp. 95-98.

[1] These researches were supported in part by a grant to the University of Wisconsin from the Atomic Energy Commission Contract No. AT(11-1)-64 and in part by the Research Committee of the Graduate School from funds supplied by the Wisconsin Alumni Research Foundation.

tigate visually motivated behavior. Experiment I, designed primarily to measure learning, involved testing three monkeys 20 trials a day (an hour or less) for 20 days on a color discrimination, with no other incentive provided than visual exploration. Experiment II, designed primarily to test strength and persistence of visual motivation, involved testing two monkeys 4 hr. a day for 5 days under visual-exploration incentive.

METHOD

Subjects

Three rhesus monkeys, no. 156, 159, and 167, served as *S*s in Experiment I, and two rhesus monkeys, no. 102 and 147, served as *S*s in Experiment II. All animals were adult and had had very extensive previous training on food-rewarded learning problems. Numbers 156, 159, 102, and 147 had been *S*s in manipulation-drive studies.

Apparatus

During testing the monkeys were housed in a wire cage 27 by 17 by 26 in. Over this cage *E* placed a box with front and top made of pressed wood and three sides covered by heavy black cloth. A 25-w. lamp was fastened on the roof of the box to provide illumination within. Two doors measuring 3¾ by 4 in. were fastened, flush, to the front of the box, with their bases 12 in. above the floor and 5 in. apart, center to center. Each door could be locked by a wooden pin, and each locking device contained a leaf switch connected to a 6-v. battery. When the door was pushed, contact was made with the locking device and an electric circuit was completed, illuminating a small signal light mounted on the front of the apparatus. Transparent Lucite plates 3 in. by 3 in. were mounted on the inside face of each door so as to permit differentially colored stimulus cards to be inserted between the Lucite plate and the door. An opaque screen, which could be raised or lowered by *E*, separated *S* from the stimulus cards. The apparatus stood on a table in the entrance room of the Wisconsin primate laboratory. The temperature in the test room ranged from

70° to 80°F. The temperature within the test box increased 6° to 7°F. above room temperature during the 4-hr. test sessions.

Procedure

Preliminary training. During preliminary training both doors, with neither holding a stimulus card, were closed, and one of the doors was always left unlocked, the position of the unlocked door on successive trials being determined by a sequence balanced for positional frequency. The *E* initiated each trial by raising the opaque screen and exposing the doors to the animal. If the monkey pushed against and opened the unlocked door, it was permitted 30 sec. to view the surroundings. The *E* then lowered the screen, ending the trial. If it pushed against the locked door, *S* was allowed 5 min. to try the other door. At the end of this time the door was opened by *E* for 30 sec., the screen then lowered, and the trial concluded. The intertrial period was always 30 sec. Preliminary training consisted of 20 trials a day for two days.

Discrimination training. In Experiment I the *S*s were tested on a yellow-blue discrimination, blue being the positive stimulus for monkeys 159 and 167, and yellow the positive stimulus for monkey 156. The position of the positive and negative cards followed a predetermined balanced order.

The animals were placed in the apparatus for 5 min. each day before testing began. The *E* initiated each trial by raising the opaque screen, exposing the stimulus cards. If *S* pushed open the door containing the positive stimulus, it was allowed 30 sec. of visual exploration before the screen was lowered. If *S* pushed against the door with the negative card, the door engaged the locking device, illuminating the signal light, and the screen was immediately lowered. The intertrial interval was always 30 sec., during which the stimulus cards were either rearranged or removed and returned to their previous position. A noncorrection technique was used throughout. Each animal received 20 trials a day, 5 days a week, for a total of 20 days. The time of the day for testing was not held constant. The response measures recorded were errors and response latencies, defined as time between *E*'s raising the screen and *S*'s responding to a door. The testing procedures for Experiment II were the same as those described for Experiment I except that the *S*s were tested continuously 4 hr. a day for five days with a day's rest between days 3 and 4 only. The blue card was positive for monkey 102 and the yellow card positive for monkey 147.

During both experiments people were frequently in the test room for a part of each session. When *S* opened the door, *E*, after recording the data for the trial, usually walked around the room, opened cabinets, or stepped outside the building within the 30-sec. period. Thus, the animals ordinarily were provided with a diversified environment in which several activities occurred and which offered auditory as well as visual stimulation. Care was taken to prevent the monkeys from seeing either food or other monkeys during the test sessions.

RESULTS

Experiment I

The mean percentage of correct responses made by the three monkeys is shown in Figure 1 and clearly

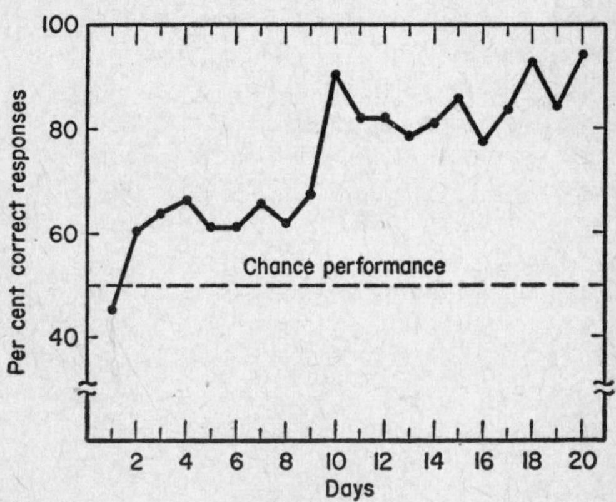

Fig. 1. Discrimination learning to visual-exploration incentives.

demonstrates learning. Animals 156, 159, and 167 attained 17 correct responses in 20 trials (performance significantly better than chance at the .01 confidence level) on days 7, 10, and 12, respectively, and they equaled or exceeded this level on 11, 7, and 2 succeeding days, respectively.

Figure 2 shows the mean log response latencies made

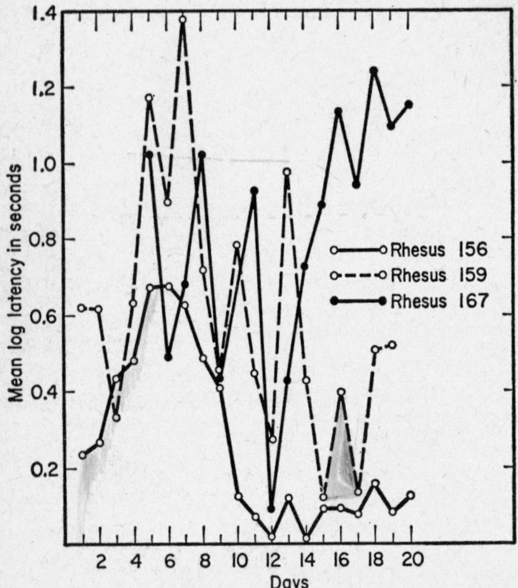

Fig. 2. Response latencies to visual-exploration incentives.

by the three monkeys on the 20 test days. Response latencies for animal 156 increase during learning and then drop to, and are maintained at, a low level. Similar results except for greater interday variability are obtained for animal 159. Response latencies for animal 167 increase during the second half of the experiment.

Experiment II

The individual discrimination-learning curves for the two Ss of the second experiment are plotted in Figure 3.

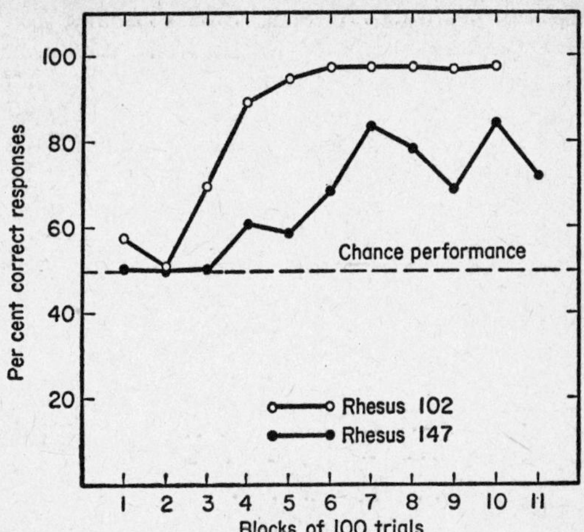

Fig. 3. Discrimination learning to visual-exploration incentives.

Number 102 attains and then maintains almost perfect performance; no. 147 performs consistently during the last 600 trials at a level significantly better than chance at the .01 confidence level.

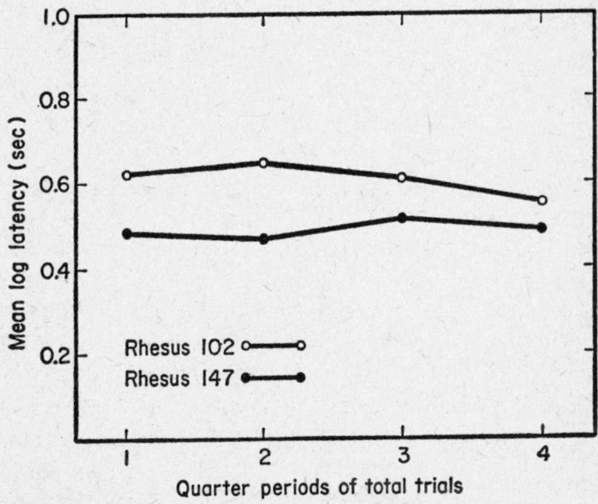

Fig. 4. Response latencies within test periods.

Figure 4 shows the mean log response latencies within test periods. The total trials made by each animal each day were divided into fourths of total daily trials and then averaged for all five days. These data show that the animals responded at a relatively constant and rapid rate throughout the 4-hr. test sessions. The data of Figure 5

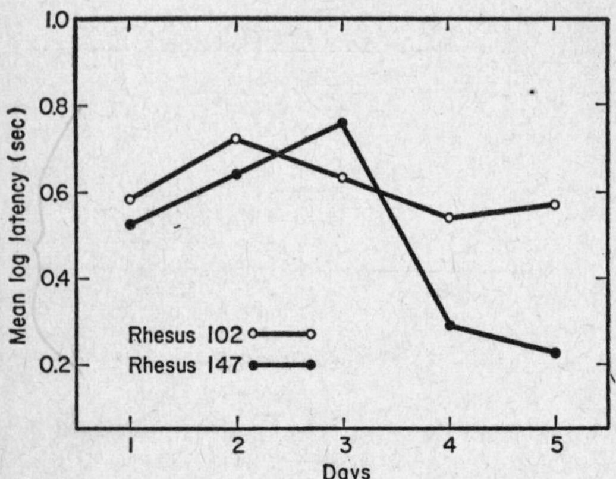

Fig. 5. Response latencies as a function of days.

give no indication of increasing response latencies during the course of the five days of testing. The response latencies for monkey 147 actually are at their lowest on days 4 and 5.

Additional Performance Measures

Although records of vocalization and cage-shaking had not been planned and were not systematically made, the *E*s were impressed by the extreme paucity of vocalizations. The monkeys appeared to be quieter in the test situation than in their home cages or standard laboratory test rooms. Only monkeys 147 and 167 shook their cages, 167 infrequently, 147 more often. Cage-shaking was certainly no more frequent than in the home situation. Monkey 147 was a mature and unusually large, violent, aggressive male.

Defecation was not frequent in any animal except no.

159, and amount of defecation, commonly and appropriately accepted as a measure of emotionality in monkeys, tended to decrease during the course of the experiment.

DISCUSSION

These experiments demonstrate beyond question that monkeys can learn object discriminations and maintain their performance at a high level of efficiency with visual-exploration reward.

The persistence of visual-exploratory motives throughout long daily test sessions and throughout series of daily test sessions also testifies to the importance, strength, and persistence of these motives elicited by external stimuli. Monkeys 156 and 159 show little or no decrease in motivational strength as indicated by response latency measures throughout 20 days of testing in Experiment I (see Fig. 2). Similarly, monkeys 102 and 147 show no decrease in motivational strength either during test days (see Fig. 4) or on successive test days (see Fig. 5) in Experiment II.

The efficient maintenance of visual-exploration motivational strength in these animals argues strongly against any explanation in terms of secondary reinforcement, for second-order conditioned responses not based on unconditioned pain responses tend to extinguish rapidly. The lack of evidence of disturbed behavior—either somatic responses of vocalization or violence, or visceral responses of defecation—would appear to render any explanation of this behavior in terms of anxiety improbable unless one wishes to define anxiety in terms of any and all conditions of deprivation.

The most obvious and acceptable explanation for the observed performances of the monkeys lies in the hypothesis that monkeys—and presumably all primates—have a strong motive toward visual exploration of their environment and that learning may be established on the basis of this motive just as it may be established on the basis of any motive that regularly and reliably elicits responses.

CONCLUSIONS

1. Five rhesus monkeys learned a discrimination problem on the basis of a visual-exploration incentive.

2. Efficient performance was maintained during the long daily sessions and throughout a series of daily sessions with little or no evidence of satiation.

3. A visual-exploration motive is hypothesized on the basis of the obtained data, and it is suggested that this motive is strong, persistent, and not derived from, or conditioned upon, other motivational or drive states.

REFERENCES

1. DAVIS, R. T., SETTLAGE, P. H., & HARLOW, H. F. Performance of normal and brain-operated monkeys on mechanical puzzles with and without food incentive. *J. Genet. Psychol.*, 1950, **77**, 305-311.
2. GATELY, M. J. Manipulation drive in experimentally naive rhesus monkeys. Unpublished master's thesis, Univer. of Wisconsin, 1950.
3. HARLOW, H. F. Learning and satiation of response in intrinsically motivated complex puzzle performance by monkeys. *J. comp. physiol. Psychol.*, 1950, **43**, 289-294.
4. HARLOW, H. F., HARLOW, MARGARET K., & MEYER, D. F. Learning motivated by a manipulation drive. *J. exp. Psychol.*, 1950, **40**, 228-234.
5. HARLOW, H. F., & MCCLEARN, G. E. Object discriminations learned by monkeys on the basis of manipulation motives. *J. comp. physiol. Psychol.*, in press.

12

Failure to Find a Learned Drive Based on Hunger; Evidence for Learning Motivated by "Exploration"[1]

ARLO K. MYERS AND NEAL E. MILLER

Yale University

This paper reports two experiments. The first attempts to show that hungry rats rewarded by food will acquire a learned drive. The second explains certain paradoxical results of the first by showing that animals satiated on food and water will learn a new habit in order, apparently, to get the chance to explore and/or exercise.

Miller (11, 12) has presented a paradigm for showing that previously neutral stimuli have acquired learned drive value by demonstrating that they will motivate the learning of a new habit. An experiment on fear (11) used relatively massed trials in an apparatus consisting of a black and a white compartment separated by a sliding door. Rats were motivated by a shock in the white compartment to run through the door, which opened in front of them, and were rewarded by escaping the shock as soon as they entered the black compartment. After they had learned, they were given trials without the primary drive of pain from electric shock. During these trials without primary drive, they learned two new habits (first to rotate a wheel and then to press a bar)

This article originally appeared in the *Journal of Comparative and Physiological Psychology*, 47, 1954, pp. 428-436.

[1] This investigation was supported by a research grant, M647, from the National Institute of Mental Health, of the National Institutes of Health, Public Health Service. The main findings were presented at the April 1954 meeting of the Eastern Psychological Association at New York.

in order to escape from the white compartment. Before any training, they had shown no definite preference for the black compartment; control animals that had received similar training with a much weaker electric shock did not learn (12, p. 448). Therefore, it was concluded (*a*) that the white compartment was a neutral cue before its association with strong shock, and (*b*) that the learned drive (presumably fear) could motivate the acquisition of a new habit in exactly the same way as could hunger or any other primary drive.

In an additional experiment, Miller (10) compared a learned drive based on hunger with one based on electric shock. A new group of fear rats was trained in the way that has just been described; the other group was trained under 22-hr. hunger (superimposed on a restricted diet) to run from the white compartment to secure food in the black one, and then, after hunger had been satiated, was tested for new learning—pressing a bar to open the door. In this experiment, which used relatively massed trials, the fear animals learned to press the bar but the hunger ones did not. The failure of the hunger animals to learn in the test trials of this experiment serves as an additional control for factors such as innate preference for the black compartment or exploratory drive. But E. E. Anderson's (1) study of the "externalization of drive" suggests that a learned drive, initially based on hunger and rewarded by food, may be used to motivate new learning in satiated animals. The fact that Anderson used distributed trials (one a day), might account for the difference between his results and Miller's.

A study by Calvin, Bicknell, and Sperling (5) presents a different type of evidence which is interpreted as showing a learned drive based on hunger. The different measure used in this study is the amount of food eaten by moderately hungry animals in the presence of a stimulus that had been associated either with stronger hunger or with satiation. This study also used distributed trials.

EXPERIMENT I

The purpose of this experiment was (*a*) to repeat, with trials distributed one per day, Miller's attempt to use hunger to establish a learned drive capable of motivating satiated animals to learn a new habit, (*b*) to see if Anderson's (1) general procedure would produce learned drive in Miller's apparatus, and (*c*) to study the effect on the acquisition of the learned drive of different numbers of training trials motivated by the primary drive of hunger and rewarded by food.

Method

Subjects. The *Ss* were 36 naive male albino rats of the Sprague-Dawley strain, 70 to 90 days old at the start of the experiment. They were housed in individual cages throughout the experiment.

Apparatus. The animals were run in Miller's learned drive apparatus, the essential features of which have been illustrated elsewhere (6, 11, 12). This consists of an enclosure 9 in. high by 6 in. wide by 48 in. long which is divided by a guillotine door into two compartments each 24 in. long. One compartment is painted white and has a grid floor, while the other is black with a solid floor of black metal. The front wall of both compartments is glass, allowing *E* to observe *S*. Each compartment contains a small socket hole in the rear wall about 4 in. above the floor and ¾ in. away from the guillotine door. A cylindrical brass rod ¼ in. in diameter may be inserted into either socket so that it protrudes 1 in. In Experiment I the bar was present at all times in the white compartment only.

The floor of the white compartment was hinged, so that when *E* placed *S* into it, a slight movement down closed a contact which started a Springfield timer. When it made the proper response (either touching the door or the bar, depending on how a switch was set), *S* completed a circuit to the grid floor so that a sub-threshold current actuated a vacuum tube relay which stopped the timer and allowed the door to drop open.

A separate "activity box" apparatus was used to try to satiate any activity before test trials. It consisted of an open-topped rectangular enclosure 60 in. long by 30 in. wide by 24 in. high. Two additional walls bisected the length and width of this enclosure, dividing it into four identical compartments. To increase the opportunity for activity, the floor of each of these compartments was divided into four spaces by three parallel partitions 4 in. high.

Procedure. To insure a high level of hunger throughout drive-acquisition training, the animals were given only 1-hr. access to Purina Laboratory Checkers each day after water had been temporarily removed.

Taming was begun five days before the beginning of the experiment proper. Once a day, ½ hr. before the feeding time, each animal was picked up from its home cage and placed in another small cage which contained a small, 3-gm. pellet of wet ground Purina Chow. After eating the pellet, *S* was returned to the home cage.

Four groups, approximately equated for mean body weight, were randomly assigned to four experimental conditions: 70 trials, 30 trials, 10 trials, and 0 trials of drive-acquisition training.

The 70-trial group began training in the learned drive apparatus immediately, while the 30- and 10-trial groups were started 40 and 60 days later, respectively. Thus all three groups finished their training and were tested at the same time. Training trials were given one per day, so that drive-acquisition training required 70 days. In order that the taming, feeding, and handling experiences of animals in all four groups would be approximately the same, those groups *not* being run in the apparatus during these 70 days were removed from their home cages, fed a 3-gm. pellet of wet mash in another cage, and returned to the home cage once a day.

The drive-acquisition trials were run as follows: An animal was taken from its home cage and placed in the white compartment. In order to attach the response to as great a variety of orientational cues as possible, the animals were placed on odd-numbered trials at the far end of the compartment facing the closed door, and on even-numbered trials, in the middle of the compartment facing away from the door. When placed inside *S* started the timer. When *S* touched the door, *S* stopped the timer, caused the door to drop open, and could enter the black compartment and eat the pellet which was on a small metal plate in the center of the floor. The rat was allowed to remain in the black compartment for 1 min. and then was gently lifted out and returned to the home cage. If it had not finished eating the pellet, *S* was allowed to carry it to the home cage. All animals learned to do this within four or five trials; before that *E* carried any uneaten portion to the rat's cage with *S*.

To facilitate learning and reduce initial fear, on the first trial the door was left open, and on the second trial the door was dropped as soon as the rat was within 8 in. of it.

The time for the animal to drop the door was recorded to the nearest .01 sec. for each trial. To normalize the distribution, the times were converted into speed scores by the formula $X = 100/t$. Since the animals were started from different orientations in the compartment on odd and even trials, scores were averaged over blocks of two trials.

After the 70-day drive-acquisition training, all animals were placed on an ad lib. diet of water and Purina Laboratory Checkers for the remainder of the experiment. They were allowed two weeks to recover from any effects of deprivation or "satiation shock." Then the second phase of the experiment, the test for learned drive, commenced.

All traces of food were removed from the apparatus. To insure complete satiation during these trials, each animal was given a supply of wet mash for 48 min. before its daily run in the apparatus. To minimize any exercise or activity drive during the test, each animal was placed, before its daily trial, in the activity box, where it could run and climb over the low partitions and eat bits of wet mash which were scattered about the floor.

Each animal went through the following routine: 28 min. with wet mash in the home cage; 16 min. with wet mash in the activity box; 4 min. more with wet mash in the home cage; then a test trial in the apparatus. In the extremely rare event that an animal was still eating when it was time for *E* to pick *S* up for a trial, *S* was given enough time to finish eating.

During the test trials, animals were always placed in the far end of the apparatus facing the door. The control of dropping the door was transferred from touching the door to touching the bar, which had always been present.

There was no food in the apparatus. In order to cope with unusually long trials and eventual extinction, animals that had not touched the bar within 2 min. on any trial were removed to the detention cage. Animals that did press the bar were given a maximum of 1 min. in which to cross into the black compartment with all four feet so that the door could be closed by sliding it up. If an animal failed to enter within 1 min., it was removed to the detention cage. If it entered the black compartment, *S* remained there for 30 sec. and then was removed to the detention cage. After being in the detention cage for 8 min., all animals were returned to the home cage. The detention cage was used as a precaution against any reward effect of an immediate return to the home cage after removal from the black compartment.

All four groups were given 30 daily trials on the new task of pressing the bar. The latency of bar pressing was recorded and transformed into a speed score.

Results

Figure 1 shows the learning of the door-touching response. All three groups learned readily. The 30- and

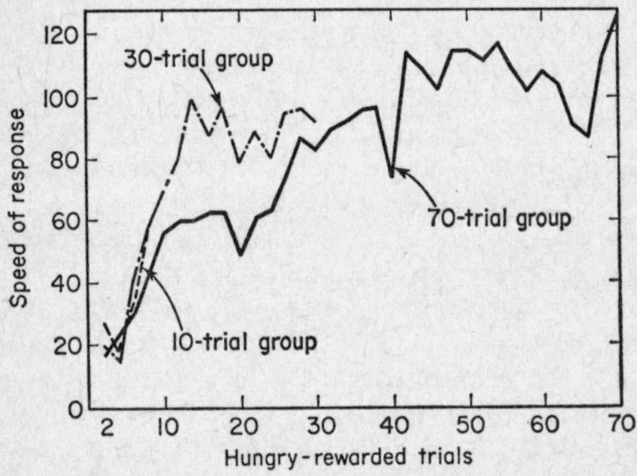

Fig. 1. Learning of the door-touching response by groups given various numbers of trials in the drive-acquisition apparatus. Speed of response = 100/*time in sec. Trials plotted by pairs. The 30- and 10-trial groups had respectively 40 and 60 more days than the 70-trial group of preliminary handling and feeding while on the deprivation schedule.*

10-trial groups seemed to learn somewhat more rapidly than the 70-trial group, the 30-trial group being significantly superior for the sum of the first 30 trials ($p = .02$). The additional taming, handling, and feeding which the 10- and 30-trial groups had received before the beginning of training may have reduced their initial fear below that of the 70-trial group or may have given the food pellet additional secondary reward value.

Figure 2 shows how all four groups learn the new

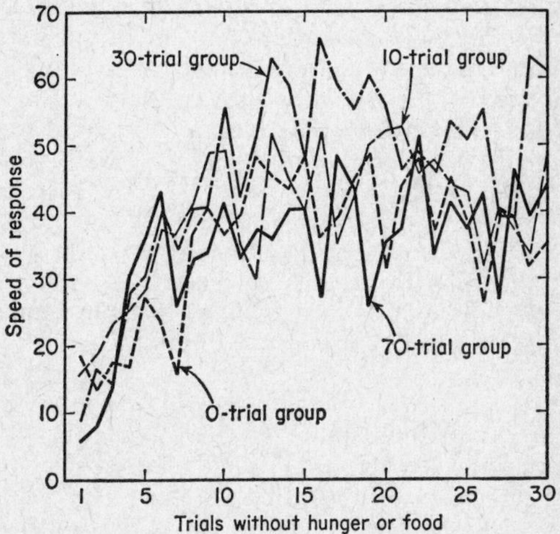

Fig. 2. Learning of the new bar-pressing response during trials without hunger drive and food reward by groups which had previously had various numbers of hungry and rewarded trials in the apparatus. Speed of response = 100/time in sec.

response of touching the bar when tested during the second phase of the experiment without the primary drive of hunger. All four groups show a definite learning curve; there are no reliable differences among them. Each animal's scores were summed for the first ten, middle ten, and last ten trials, and the resulting matrix of 108 scores for the 36 animals were used in an analysis of variance. The variance due to blocks of trials (learning) was highly significant ($p < .01$), while the differences among groups and the groups × trials interaction did not even approach significance. Thus it is clear that all groups learned, but there were no significant differences either in mean performance or in learning rate among the experimental groups. A further analysis of the blocks of trials variable shows that the differences between the first and second block and between the first and third block are highly significant ($p < .01$). Though there is a slight downward trend from the second to the third block, it is not significant ($p = .68$).

Finally, it should be noted that even the small differences that do exist among the four groups are not systematically related to the number of trials during drive-acquisition training. In mean speed of bar pressing, the four groups rank as follows: 30-trial, 0-trial, 70-trial, and 10-trial.

Discussion

The rats in the present experiment learned, irrespective of whether or not they had received previous drive-acquisition training. Does this mean that the animals in Miller's (10, 11, 12) previous studies of fear (described in the introduction to this paper) would have learned without any fear-acquisition training? Two control groups were involved in those studies composed of rats which had been given drive-acquisition training with either hunger (10) or weak electric shock (12, p. 448), respectively. Since neither control group showed any subsequent learning, it was concluded that drive-acquisition training with strong electric shock (presumably arousing fear) was essential for learning under the conditions of those experiments.

But why did the control animals in those experiments fail to learn the new habit of bar pressing while the animals in the present experiment did learn it? It is conceivable that the weak shock induced crouching or some other habit incompatible with subsequent learning, and that those animals would have learned if they had been run without any previous shock. In that case Miller's previous experiments would not be a valid demonstration of motivation by fear and reward by reduction in fear. It is difficult to imagine, however, why a *weak* shock should produce *more* interference with learning than the strong shock which did lead to subsequent learning. Furthermore, the control animals given drive-acquisition training with hunger failed to learn in the previous experiment but did learn in the present one. This suggests that the different results must have been produced by the one consistent difference in procedure, namely the spacing of the trials. In the previous experiment the trials were relatively massed, at 3-min. intervals, while in the present one they were widely distributed, one a day. It would seem that during spaced trials in our apparatus rats will learn without previous drive-acquisition training, but that during massed trials they will not learn unless they are motivated by some reasonably strong drive, such as fear established by painful electric shocks.

Since this assumption about the effects of massing the trials is so crucial to the interpretation of the previous experiments on fear, it will be tested further in the second experiment in this paper.

The rats in the 70-trial group in our experiment showed definite learning comparable to that of the rats in Anderson's (1) experimental group which was also run with trials spaced one a day. But this learning could not be attributed to *learned* drive in our experiment since the rats with no trials of drive acquisition learned equally well. Anderson's control rats also showed some learning. Since he does not present any tests of statistical reliability, it is possible that the fairly impressive difference between the means of his experimental and control groups was due to chancc. It is also possible that the difference was reliable but was an artifact of interfering factors, such as fear of the maze and handling, which may not have been eliminated as completely for his control animals as for his experimental ones. His control animals were habituated in a shorter maze than the one used for pretraining the experimental animals. Furthermore, the feeding which was associated with the handling of the experimental animals may have helped to extinguish their interfering fears. In other words, the function of this feeding may have been not to externalize drive, but to reduce conflict. On the other hand, it is possible that the more complex task which Anderson used provided conditions which were more favorable either for acquiring learned drive or for measuring it. While our results do not disprove Anderson's conclusions, they cast some doubt on them and set a limit to the generality of their application.

Similar questions arise about the purported demonstration of learned hunger by Calvin *et al.* (5). Their conditions may have been more favorable than ours either because (*a*) eating may be a more sensitive measure than learning, (*b*) conditioning a drive may require the association of an *increase* in drive intensity with the to-be-conditioned stimuli (a state of affairs more probable in their experiment than ours), or (*c*) the close association with drive reduction in the black compartment of our apparatus may have produced an anticipatory relaxation which neutralized any learned drive in the white compartment (12, p. 451). Or possibly the difference between the two groups in their experiment came from a nausea conditioned to the cues during their association with satiation in the control group rather than from appetite conditioned to the cues during their association with hunger in the experimental group.

The most striking result of our experiment was the rapid learning of the new habit of bar pressing by the satiated and apparently nonrewarded animals irrespective of whether or not they had previous drive-acquisition training. Why do these animals, especially those in the 0-trial group, learn to press the bar? It seems possible that explanations could be developed in terms of light avoidance, exploratory drive, activity drive, curiosity, or Guthrie's (7) concept of stimulus change as a protection from retroactive inhibition. Conceivably the more conventional sources of primary or learned reward operated in some subtle fashion, but such factors had supposedly been reduced to a minimum both by satiating the animals and by delaying the handling and return to the home cage for some time after the bar was pressed. In an attempt to test some of these hypotheses, a second experiment was performed.

EXPERIMENT II

The purpose of the second experiment was to determine some of the conditions that are necessary for the learning which was observed in the first experiment. In order to test the hypothesis that the extensive handling, taming, and feeding of the 0-trial group was responsible for their learning, all rats were given briefer taming while satiated and without any food reward. To test the hypothesis of preference for the black compartment (e.g., from light avoidance), the first group was run from white to black while the second one was run in the *opposite* direction. This symmetrical type of a control for obvious, or even latent, preference is believed to be a particularly important one for experiments purporting to demonstrate learning from a motivation such as exploratory behavior, curiosity, or activity drive. To determine whether the sight and sound of the door dropping is sufficient to produce learning or whether entering and inspecting the black compartment is necessary, a third group was run from the white compartment but with a white panel fastened securely in place just behind the door. To determine whether spaced practice was necessary, a fourth group was run with massed trials. So that the massing would be comparable to that used in Miller's (10, 11) experiments on fear, it was necessary to eliminate the 16 min. in the activity box and 8 min. in the detention cage. In order to control for these changes in procedure, a fifth group was run with spaced trials, but with the periods in the activity box and detention cage omitted.

Method

Subjects. The Ss were 50 naive male albino rats of the Sprague-Dawley strain, approximately 70 days old at the start of the experiment. All animals were maintained in individual cages on an ad lib. diet of water and Purina Laboratory Checkers.

Apparatus. The apparatus was identical with that used in Experiment I except for minor changes. For the animals running from the black compartment, pressure on its floor started the timer; touching a bar located in the same relative position as the one in the white compartment dropped the door and stopped the timer. In other words, the operations of running from white to black or black to white were similar.

Procedure. The animals were tamed by being handled once a day for five days when satiated *without* receiving any food reward. The first phase of Experiment I, hungry-reward training in the apparatus, was omitted. The animals were on ad lib. feeding throughout the experiment, and were fed wet mash for 48 min. before each training trial. Immediately after taming, the animals were divided into five groups of ten each, approximately equated for mean body weight, and randomly assigned to the following five experimental conditions:

1. A *white-to-black group* with a procedure duplicating that used in the second phase of the first experiment.

2. A *black-to-white group* run in exactly the same way but in the opposite direction. This was the only group started in the black compartment.

3. A *white panel group* run exactly like the first group except that when the door dropped, the animals were prevented from seeing or entering the black compartment by a white wooden panel immediately behind the door. To equate the effect of the time interval between bar pressing and being picked up and placed in the detention cage, each member of this group was given a partner in the white-to-black group and was removed from the apparatus at the moment which would make *S*'s interval on that trial equal to that of its just-previously-run partner.

4. *The massed group* received all 18 of their trials in a single afternoon with an intertrial interval averaging approximately 3 min. The ten animals in this group were randomly subdivided into three, four, and three animals, respectively, which were run on the first, middle, and last days of the experiment. To achieve the close massing, the activity box and detention cage were omitted from the procedure; the animals were returned immediately to their home cages (from which food and water had been temporarily removed) after each trial. In other

respects, the procedure for the massed group was the same as that for the white-to-black group.

5. *The massed control group* was run without the activity box or detention cage to determine the effect of omitting these procedures. They were run exactly like the massed group except that their trials were distributed at the rate of one per day like those of the first three groups.

Results

All the latency scores were transformed into speed scores as described for Experiment I. The results are presented in Figure 3. The five groups start out at roughly

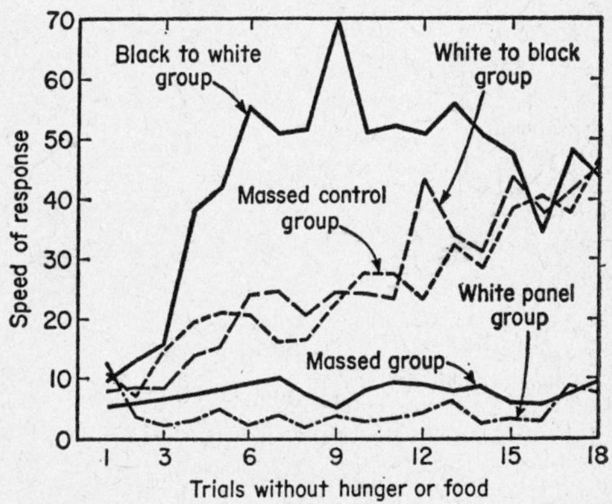

Fig. 3. Effect of experimental conditions on learning of the bar-pressing response by groups trained without hunger drive or food reward. Speed of response = 100/time in sec.

the same level of performance; although the white panel and massed groups show little change throughout the 18 trials, the others show definite learning.

Each animal's scores were summed for the first six, middle six, and last six trials, and the resulting matrix of 150 scores for the 50 animals was subjected to analysis of variance to assess the over-all effects due to blocks of trials, groups, and groups × trials interaction. All three produced highly significant *F*'s, with *p* in each case less than .01. Table 1 summarizes this analysis.

Then, for the mean of all 18 trials, separate *t* tests were computed comparing each group with every other one. Of these ten comparisons, all but two produced differences significant at the .01 level of confidence or beyond. The difference between the white-to-black and massed control groups and between the massed and white panel groups were not significant ($p = .79$ and .59, respectively).

TABLE 1

Analysis of variance of speed scores in Experiment II

Source of variance	Mean square	*df*	*F*	*p*
1. Groups	2,716,275*	4	13.86	<.01
2. Trials	865,061**	2	71.48	<.01
3. Trials × Groups	221,908**	8	18.34	<.01
4. Rats within groups	196,031	45		
5. Rats within groups × Trials	12,102	90		

* Tested against 4.
** Tested against 5.

Next, the significance of the *trend* for each group was analyzed by computing separate *t* tests among the three blocks of six trials. None of the comparisons among blocks of trials even approached significance for either the massed or white panel groups. The other three groups all showed an increase from the first to the third block of trials significant beyond the .01 level of confidence. These three groups also showed significant increases from the first to the second block, and from the second to the third block, with the exception of the black-to-white group, which showed a significant *decrement* from the second to the third block of trials.

Since all groups started from nearly the same level of performance, the foregoing analysis gives a fairly complete picture of the differences among the five groups. As a further check, separate *t* tests were computed on the differences between trends among the five groups. An examination of the resulting 30 comparisons simply confirms the impression one gets from an examination of Figure 3. There is little difference between the white-to-black and massed control groups or between the massed and white panel groups at any stage of training.

After pressing the bar, all the animals (except those prevented by the white panel) at least poked their heads into the other compartment and sniffed around. More of the animals going to the white entered all the way than of those going to the black. On the first trial, the difference between the black-to-white group and each of the others was significant beyond the .01 level.

For the first 18 trials during which a direct comparison is possible, there is little or no difference between the learning by the white-to-black group in Experiment II and by the 70-trial group (white-to-black) in Experiment I. Though the rats that had had 70 drive-acquisition trials before the test may show some slight superiority in early trials (presumably because their fear of the door's dropping has been extinguished), the mean speed for these animals averaged over all 18 trials is not significantly greater than that for the white-to-black group of Experiment II ($p = .38$).

Discussion

The main results of Experiment II were as follows: (*a*) Satiated and nonrewarded animals will learn the bar-pressing response either to open the door from the white to the black compartment or from the black to the white compartment. (*b*) Animals that pressed the bar (in the white compartment) to drop the door but were prevented from seeing or entering the other compartment did not learn. (*c*) Animals trained with massed instead of spaced trials (white-to-black) did not learn. (*d*) The failure of the massed group to learn was not due to the omission of the activity box and detention cage from their running procedure because the massed control group, which was given spaced trials with these procedures omitted, learned as well as the white-to-black group.

The fact that the black-to-white group learned faster than the white-to-black group suggests that a preference for the white compartment may be a source of some motivation and reward in the apparatus. However, the fact that both groups (running in opposite directions) learned shows that such a preference is not a necessary condition for learning. Apparently the fact that pressing the bar is followed by the chance to observe and enter a new compartment is sufficient to produce learning.

The fact that the white panel group did not learn shows that the cues produced by bar pressing and door dropping, or by being picked up and returned to the home cage via the detention cage, are not sufficient to produce learning; it suggests that the act of seeing or exploring the other compartment, or perhaps experiencing the change between the two compartments (irrespective of the direction of change), produces the reinforcement. But we cannot tell whether or not exposure to the new stimuli in the other compartment would produce learning even if the animals were prevented from entering or exploring.

Since dropping the door provided the animals with more space in which to move about, it might be argued that the reinforcement came from this greater opportunity to exercise or escape restriction. However, the white-to-black group did not seem to perform any worse than the massed control group which was run under identical conditions except for the omission of the activity box and detention cage. Presumably exercise in the activity box before each trial, as opposed to confinement in the small home cage, would have reduced the exercise drive and produced poorer performance in the white-to-black group. The fact that the massed controls were returned directly to their home cage, rather than to a detention cage, after each trial might also be expected to produce superior learning if return to the home cage were a significant part of the reinforcement. Thus, the lack of any appreciable difference between these two groups also serves as additional evidence against assigning an important role in these particular experiments to reinforcement from return to the home cage.

Guthrie's (7) principles might be used to explain the learning shown by groups that had a chance to enter the other compartment and were run with distributed practice. Pressing the bar would be the last thing that the animal did before entering the other compartment, where the change in cues would protect S from unlearning the habit of pressing the bar by removing the opportunity to perform different responses to the original cues. But this explanation—at least in its simplest, most obvious form—would seem to apply equally well to the massed group which did *not* learn. If it is assumed that general changes in posture and other sources of interoceptive stimulation are more likely to occur during the longer interval, the task of the animals with distributed practice would be more difficult, since they would have to attach the response of pressing the bar to a greater variety of combinations of cues. Thus it seems that a simple form of Guthrie-type explanation is not able to account for the difference between the learning of the groups with massed and distributed practice.

The failure of the massed group to learn confirms the conclusion from Miller's (10, 11, 12) previous studies that learning will not occur during *massed trials* in his apparatus unless specific procedures have been used to establish a learned drive, such as fear.

Though some inferiority of the massed group would be expected from the principle of reactive inhibition (9), the magnitude of the difference found in this experiment suggests that other factors may be operating. If learning were motivated by a relatively weak drive of exercise, exploration, or curiosity, it is possible that this motivation might be satiated or extinguished by the massed practice and not have enough chance to recover during the short time between trials. Montgomery (14, 15, 16) and Berlyne (2) have shown that a rat's tendency to investigate a new stimulus object decreases rapidly with continued exposure and shows little recovery during a short interval of nonexposure but considerable recovery during a 24-hr. interval. Thus, the satiation of an exploratory drive during massed trials but recovery during spaced ones may account for the difference in the second experiment. If an exploratory tendency can produce learning like other drives such as hunger, and also show a similar pattern of satiation and recovery, these functional parallels to already known drives would help to justify its classification in the same category with them, namely as a drive.[2]

A considerable body of challenging experimental work interpreted in terms of "exploratory" and "manipulatory" drives has been reported by Harlow and his associates (8). Harlow believes that these drives differ from the better-studied ones, such as hunger, in that external stimuli, i.e., the ones explored, both elicit the drive and operate as reinforcement.

We, however, would not put a drive in a special category simply because it is elicited by external stimuli. We prefer the drive-reduction hypothesis developed by Hull (9) and Miller and Dollard (13), which treats externally elicited drives (such as pain) in the same way as other drives. Furthermore, as Brown (4) has pointed out, in some of the Wisconsin studies on the "visual exploration drive" the novel stimuli to be explored are not present at the time the animal begins working to secure them. If the novel stimuli elicit the drive, this would mean that the drive is produced *after* the animal has performed the response the drive is supposed to be motivating.

If, as Harlow seems to imply, the same novel stimuli elicit an exploratory drive and *simultaneously* serve as an exploratory reward, a strict drive-reduction theory would be unable to deal with these phenomena. However, we believe it is possible that confinement produces anxiety, restraint is frustrating, or monotony arouses a drive of boredom. Indeed, the observation of small children who are required to sit absolutely still, the reports of prisoners subjected to solitary confinement, and the difficulty of Bexton, Heron, and Scott (3) in retaining Ss in their experiment on the effects of decreased sensory variation would indicate that such conditions can produce strong

[2] According to observations by Sharpless (17), novel stimuli elicit an "arousal reaction" presumably involving the brain-stem reticular formation. This "arousal reaction," indicated by characteristic changes in brain waves, shows fairly rapid extinction (presumably as the stimulus loses its novelty) and eventual recovery analogous to that described above. It is conceivable that this arousal reaction to novel stimuli is part of the mechanism of exploratory motivation.

motivation. Therefore, we suggest that drives produced by homogeneous or monotonous stimulation, enforced inaction, etc., may be reduced by sensory variety, freedom of action, etc., and that such drive reduction is the *reinforcement* involved in learning for "exploratory," "manipulatory," and "exercise" rewards. For the present, we choose the more parsimonious alternative of trying to analyze such concepts as exploratory drive along the same lines as conventional drives.

We also believe some writers have been too quick to assume that novel stimuli elicit a drive simply because such stimuli commonly elicit activity or exploration. This may well be a case of confusing the cue properties of a stimulus with possible drive properties. Exploration may be an innate response to novelty in some species, or it may occur because exploration has been reinforced in the presence of novel cues in the animal's past history. Activity is a poor measure of drive; some drives, such as fatigue or fear, may tend to decrease activity.

Irrespective of how the foregoing problems of theory and interpretation are handled, we agree that it is extremely important to develop techniques for studying significant sources of motivation which have previously been neglected. Such studies may lead to fundamental extensions or radical revisions of our present concepts. Certainly our present list of experimentally studied motives is far too short.

SUMMARY

Experiment I. Four groups of hungry rats were given 70, 30, 10, and 0 drive-acquisition trials in Miller's learned-drive apparatus with food reward in the goal compartment. The animals were started in the white compartment and learned to touch the door to open it and run into the black compartment containing the food. In a subsequent test for learned drive, these four groups, now satiated and nonrewarded, were required to learn the new response of pressing a bar to open the door to the goal compartment.

All four groups learned to press the bar, but there were no significant differences among the four drive-acquisition groups. The experiment (*a*) does not provide any evidence for a learned drive based on hunger and food reward, and (*b*) shows that rats with no prior experience in the apparatus will learn to press the bar while satiated and without the reward of food.

There is a brief discussion of possible artifacts in previous experiments purporting to show a learned drive based on hunger.

Experiment II. Rats satiated for food and water were trained in the learned-drive apparatus to press the bar in one compartment to gain access, through the door, to the other compartment. No food or water reward was present in the apparatus at any time.

It was found that: (*a*) Animals will learn to press the bar either to gain entry to the black compartment from the white one, or vice versa. (*b*) Animals that responded in the white compartment but were not allowed to see or enter the black compartment did not learn. (*c*) Animals trained (in the white-to-black situation) with massed instead of spaced trials did not learn.

A simple application of Guthrie's concept of stimulus change as a basis for a persisting habit does not seem to be able to explain the marked difference between the groups with massed and distributed practice. Explanations in terms of exploratory or activity drive are discussed.

The absence of learning during massed trials in these experiments confirms the results of two control groups used in Miller's previous experiments on fear and shows that the learning which he observed during massed trials following strong electric shocks would not have occurred without these shocks, which presumably established a strong learned drive of fear.

REFERENCES

1. ANDERSON, E. E. The externalization of drive: III. Maze learning by non-rewarded and satiated rats. *J. genet. Psychol.*, 1941, **59**, 397-426.
2. BERLYNE, D. E. Novelty and curiosity as determiners of exploratory behavior. *Brit. J. Psychol.*, 1950, **41**, 68-80.
3. BEXTON, W. H., HERON, W., & SCOTT, T. H.

Effects of decreased variation in the sensory environment. *Canad. J. Psychol.*, 1954, **8**, 70-76.

4. BROWN, J. S. Problems presented by the concept of acquired drives. In *Current theory and research in motivation*. Lincoln: Univer. of Nebraska Press, 1953. Pp. 1-21.
5. CALVIN, J. S., BICKNELL, ELIZABETH ANN, & SPERLING, D. S. Establishment of a conditioned drive based on the hunger drive. *J. comp. physiol. Psychol.*, 1953, **46**, 173-175.
6. DOLLARD, J., & MILLER, N. E. *Personality and Psychotherapy: an analysis in terms of learning, thinking, and culture*. New York: McGraw-Hill, 1950.
7. GUTHRIE, E. R. *The psychology of learning*. (Rev. Ed.) New York: Harper, 1952.
8. HARLOW, H. F. Motivation as a factor in new responses. In *Current theory and research in motivation*. Lincoln: Univer. of Nebraska Press, 1953. Pp. 24-49.
9. HULL, C. L. *Principles of behavior*. New York: D. Appleton-Century, 1943.
10. MILLER, N. E. Experiments on the strength of acquired drives based on hunger. *Amer. Psychologist*, 1947, **2**, 303. (Abstract).
11. MILLER, N. E. Studies of fear as an acquirable drive: I. Fear as motivation and fear-reduction as reinforcement in the learning of new responses. *J. exp. Psychol.*, 1948, **38**, 89-101.
12. MILLER, N. E. Learnable drives and rewards. In S. S. Stevens (Ed.), *Handbook of experimental psychology*, New York: Wiley, 1951. Pp. 435-472.
13. MILLER, N. E., & DOLLARD, J. *Social learning and imitation*. New Haven: Yale Univer. Press, 1941.
14. MONTGOMERY, K. C. The relation between exploratory behavior and spontaneous alternation in the white rat. *J. comp. physiol. Psychol.*, 1951, **44**, 582-589.
15. MONTGOMERY, K. C. Exploratory behavior and its relation to spontaneous alternation in a series of maze exposures. *J. comp. physiol. Psychol.*, 1952, **45**, 50-57.
16. MONTGOMERY, K. C. Exploratory behavior as a func-

tion of "similarity" of stimulus situations. *J. comp. physiol. Psychol.*, 1953, **46**, 129-133.

17. SHARPLESS, S. Habituation of the arousal mechanism. Paper read at East. Psychol. Ass., New York, April, 1954.

13

Positive Reinforcement Produced by Electrical Stimulation of Septal Area and Other Regions of Rat Brain[1]

JAMES OLDS[2] AND PETER MILNER

McGill University

Stimuli have eliciting and reinforcing functions. In studying the former, one concentrates on the responses which come after the stimulus. In studying the latter, one looks mainly at the responses which precede it. In its reinforcing capacity, a stimulus increases, decreases, or leaves unchanged the frequency of preceding responses, and accordingly it is called a reward, a punishment, or a neutral stimulus (cf. 16).

Previous studies using chronic implantation of electrodes have tended to focus on the eliciting functions of electrical stimuli delivered to the brain (2, 3, 4, 5, 7, 10, 12, 14). The present study, on the other hand, has

The following article originally appeared in the *Journal of Comparative and Physiological Psychology*, 47, 1954, pp. 419. 427.

[1] The research reported here was made possible by grants from the Rockefeller Foundation and the National Institute of Mental Health of the U.S. Public Health Service. The authors particularly wish to express their thanks to Professor D. O. Hebb, who provided germinal ideas for the research and who backed it with enthusiastic encouragement as well as laboratory facilities and funds. The authors are also grateful to Miss Joann Feindel, who performed the histological reconstructions reported here.

[2] National Institute of Mental Health Postdoctorate Fellow of the U.S. Public Health Service.

been concerned with the reinforcing function of the electrical stimulation.[3]

METHOD

General

Stimulation was carried out by means of chronically implanted electrodes which did not interfere with the health or free behavior of *S*s to any appreciable extent. The *S*s were 15 male hooded rats, weighing approximately 250 gm. at the start of the experiment. Each *S* was tested in a Skinner box which delivered alternating current to the brain so long as a lever was depressed. The current was delivered over a loose lead, suspended from the ceiling, which connected the stimulator to the rat's electrode. The *S*s were given a total of 6 to 12 hr. of acquisition testing, and 1 to 2 hr. of extinction testing. During acquisition, the stimulator was turned on so that a response produced electrical stimulation; during extinction, the stimulator was turned off so that a response produced no electrical stimulation. Each *S* was given a percentage score denoting the proportion of his total acquisition time given to responding. This score could be compared with the animal's extinction score to determine whether the stimulation had a positive, negative, or neutral reinforcing effect. After testing, the animal was sacrificed. Its brain was frozen, sectioned, stained, and examined microscopically to determine which structure of the brain had been stimulated. This permitted correlation of acquisition scores with anatomical structures.

Electrode Implantation

Electrodes are constructed by cementing a pair of enameled silver wires of 0.010-in. diameter into a Lucite block, as shown in Figure 1. The parts of the wires which penetrate the brain are cemented together to form a needle, and this is cut to the correct length to

[3] The present preliminary paper deals mainly with methods and behavioral results. A detailed report of the locus of positive, negative, and neutral reinforcing effects of electrical brain stimulation is being prepared by the first author.

reach the desired structure in the brain. This length is determined from Krieg's rat brain atlas (11) with slight modifications as found necessary by experience. The exposed cross section of the wire is the only part of the needle not insulated from the brain by enamel; stimulation therefore occurs only at the tip. Contact with the lead from the stimulator is made through two blobs of solder on the upper ends of the electrode wires; these blobs make contact with the jaws of an alligator clip which has been modified to insulate the two jaws from

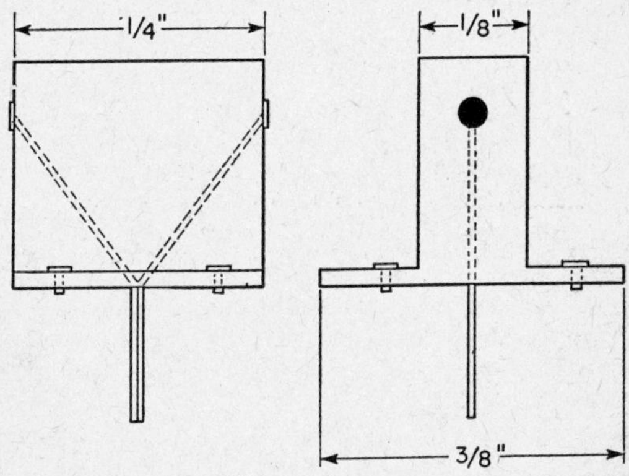

Fig. 1. Electrode design (see text for detailed description).

one another. A light, flexible hearing-aid lead connects the clip to the voltage source.

The operation of implantation is performed with the rat under Nembutal anesthesia (0.88 cc/Kg) and held in a Johnson-Krieg stereotaxic instrument (11). A midline incision is made in the scalp and the skin held out of the way by muscle retractors. A small hole is drilled in the skull with a dental burr at the point indicated by the stereotaxic instrument for the structure it is desired to stimulate. The electrode, which is clamped into the needle carrier of the instrument, is lowered until the flange of the Lucite block rests firmly on the skull. Four screw holes are then drilled in the skull through four fixing holes in the flange, and the electrode, still clamped firmly in the instrument, is fastened to the skull with jeweler's screws which exceed the diameter of the screw holes in the skull by 0.006 in. The electrode is then released from the clamp and the scalp wound closed with silk sutures. The skin is pulled tightly around the base of the Lucite block and kept well away from the contact plates. A recovery period of three days is allowed after the operation before testing.

Testing

The testing apparatus consisted of a large-levered Skinner box 11 in. long, 5 in. wide, and 12 in. high. The top was open to allow passage for the stimulating lead. The lever actuated a microswitch in the stimulating circuit so that when it was depressed, the rat received electrical stimulation. The current was obtained from the 60-cycle power line, through a step-down transformer, and was adjustable between 0 and 10 v. r.m.s. by means of a variable potentiometer. In the experiments described here the stimulation continued as long as the lever was pressed, though for some tests a time-delay switch was incorporated which cut the current off after a predetermined interval if the rat continued to hold the lever down. Responses were recorded automatically on paper strip.

On the fourth day after the operation rats were given a pretesting session of about an hour in the boxes. Each rat was placed in the box and on the lever by *E* with the stimulus set at 0.5 v. During the hour, stimulation voltage was varied to determine the threshold of a "just noticeable" effect on the rat's behavior. If the animal did not respond regularly from the start, it was placed on the lever periodically (at about 5-min. intervals). Data collected on the first day were not used in later calculations. On subsequent days, Ss were placed in the box for about 3½ hr. a day; these were 3 hr. of acquisition and ½ hr. of extinction. During the former, the rats were allowed to stimulate themselves with a voltage which was just high enough to produce some noticeable response in the resting animal. As this threshold voltage fluctuated with the passage of time, *E* would make a determination of it every half hour, unless *S* was responding regularly. At the beginning of each acquisition period, and after each voltage test, the animal was placed on the lever once by *E*. During extinction periods, conditions were precisely the same except that a bar press produced no electrical stimulation. At the beginning of each extinction period, animals which were not responding regularly were placed on the lever once by *E*. At first, rats were tested in this way for four days, but as there appeared to be little difference between the results on different days, this period was reduced to three and then to two days for subsequent animals. Thus, the first rats had about 12 hr. of acquisition after pretesting whereas later rats had about 6 hr. However, in computing the scores in our table, we have used only the first 6 hr. of acquisition for all animals, so the scores are strictly comparable. In behavioral curves, we have shown the full 12 hr. of acquisition on the earlier animals so as to illustrate the stability of the behavior over time.

At no time during the experiment were the rats deprived of food or water, and no reinforcement was used except the electrical stimulus.

Animals were scored on the percentage of time which they spent bar pressing regularly during acquisition. In order to find how much time the animal would spend in the absence of reward or punishment, a similar score was computed for periods of extinction. This extinction score provided a base line. When the acquisition score is above the extinction score, we have reward; when it is below the extinction score, we have punishment.

In order to determine percentage scores, periods when the animal was responding regularly (at least one response every 30 sec.) were counted as periods of responding; i.e., *intervals of 30 sec. or longer without a response were counted as periods of no responding.* The percentage scores were computed as the proportion of total acquisition or extinction time given to periods of responding.

Determination of Locus

On completion of testing, animals were perfused with physiological saline, followed by 10 per cent formalin.

The brains were removed, and after further fixation in formalin for about a week, frozen sections 40 microns thick were cut through the region of the electrode track. These were stained with cresyl violet and the position of the electrode tip determined.

RESULTS

Locus

In Table 1, acquisition and extinction scores are correlated with electrode placements. Figure 4 presents the acquisition scores again, this time on three cross-sec-

TABLE 1

Acquisition and extinction scores for all animals together with electrode placements and threshold voltages used during acquisition tests

Animal's no.	Locus of electrode	Stimulation voltage r.m.s.	Percentage of acquisition time spent responding	Percentage of extinction time spent responding
32	septal	2.2-2.8	75	18
34	septal	1.4	92	6
M-1	septal	1.7-4.8	85	21
M-4	septal	2.3-4.8	88	13
40	c.c.	.7-1.1	6	3
41	caudate	.9-1.2	4	4
31	cingulate	1.8	37	9
82	cingulate	.5-1.8	36	10
36	hip.	.8-2.8	11	14
3	m.l.	.5	0	4
A-5	m.t.	1.4	71	9
6	m.g.	.5	0	31
11	m.g.	.5	0	21
17	teg.	.7	2	1
9	teg.	.5	77	81

Key: *c.c.*, *corpus callosum; hip.*, hippocampus; *m.l.*, medial lemniscus; *m.t.*, Mammillothalamic tract; *m.g.*, medial geniculate; *teg.*, tegmentum.

tional maps of the rat brain, one at the forebrain level, one at the thalamic level, and one at the mid-brain level. The position of a score on the map indicates the electrode placement from which this acquisition score was obtained.

The highest scores are found together in the central portion of the forebrain. Beneath the *corpus callosum* and between the two lateral ventricles in section I of Figure 4, we find four acquisition scores ranging from 75 to 92 per cent. This is the septal area. The Ss which produced these scores are numbered 32, 34, M-1, and M-4 in Table 1. It will be noticed that while all of them spent more than 75 per cent of their acquisition time responding, they all spent less than 22 per cent of their extinction time responding. Thus the electrical stimulus in the septal area has an effect which is apparently equivalent to that of a conventional primary reward as far as the maintenance of a lever-pressing response is concerned.

If we move outside the septal area, either in the direction of the caudate nucleus (across the lateral ventricle) or in the direction of the *corpus callosum*, we find acquisition scores drop abruptly to levels of from 4 to 6 per cent. These are definitely indications of neutral (neither rewarding nor punishing) effects.

However, above the *corpus callosum* in the cingulate cortex we find an acquisition score of 37 per cent. As the extinction score in this case was 9 per cent, we may say that stimulation was rewarding.

At the thalamic level (section II of Fig. 4) we find a 36 per cent acquisition score produced by an electrode placed again in the cingulate cortex, an 11 per cent score produced by an electrode placed in the hippocampus, a 71 per cent score produced by an electrode placed exactly in the mammillothalamic tract, and a zero per cent score produced by an electrode placed in the medial lemniscus. The zero denotes negative reinforcement.

At the mid-brain level (section III of Fig. 4) there are two zero scores produced by electrodes which are in the posterior portion of the medial geniculate bodies; here again, the scores indicate a negative effect, as the

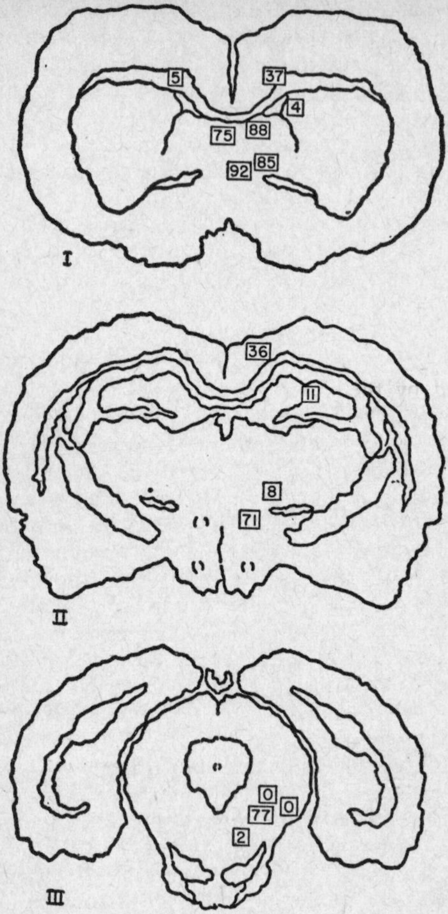

Fig. 4. Maps of three sections. (I) through the forebrain, (II) through the thalamus, (III) through the mid-brain of the rat. Boxed numbers give acquisition percentage scores produced by animals with electrodes stimulating at these points. On section I the acquisition scores 75, 88, 92, 85 fall in the septal forebrain area. On the same section there is a score of 4 in the caudate nucleus, a score of 6 in the white matter below the cortex, and a score of 37 in the medial (cingulate) cortex.

corresponding extinction scores are 31 and 21 per cent. There is an electrode deep in the medial, posterior tegmentum which produces a 2 per cent score; this seems quite neutral, as the extinction score in this case is 1 per cent. Finally, there is an electrode shown on this section which actually stands 1½ mm. anterior to the point where it is shown; it was between the red nucleus and the posterior commissure. It produced an acquisition score of 77 per cent, but an extinction score of 81 per cent. This must be a rewarding placement, but the high extinction score makes it difficult to interpret.

Behavior

We turn our attention briefly to the behavioral data produced by the more rewarding electrode placements.

The graph in Figure 5 is a smoothed cumulative response curve illustrating the rate of responding of rat No. 32 (the lowest-scoring septal area rat) during acquisition and extinction. The animal gave a total of slightly over 3000 responses in the 12 hr. of acquisition. When the current was turned on, the animal responded at a rate of 285 responses an hour; when the current was turned off, the rate fell close to zero.

The graph in Figure 6 gives similar data on rat No. 34 (the highest-scoring septal rat). The animal stimulated itself over 7500 times in 12 hr. Its average response rate during acquisition was 742 responses an hour; during extinction, practically zero.

Figure 7 presents an unsmoothed cumulative response curve for one day of responding for rat No. A-5. This is to illustrate in detail the degree of control exercised by the electrical reward stimulus. While this rat was actually bar pressing, it did so at 1920 responses an hour; that is, about one response for every 2 sec. During the first period of the day it responded regularly while on acquisi-

---

On section II the acquisition score of 36 is in the medial (cingulate) cortex, 11 is in the hippocampus, 71 is in the mammillothalamic tract, and 0 is in the medical lemniscus. On section III the two zeroes are in the medial geniculate, 2 is in the tegmental reticular substance, 77 falls 2 mm. anterior to the section shown. It is between the posterior commissure and the red nucleus.

tion, extinguished very rapidly when the current was turned off, and reconditioned readily when the current was turned on again. At reconditioning points, *E* gave *S* one stimulus to show that the current was turned on again, but *E* did not place *S* on the lever. During longer periods of acquisition, *S* occasionally stopped responding for short periods, but in the long run *S* spent almost

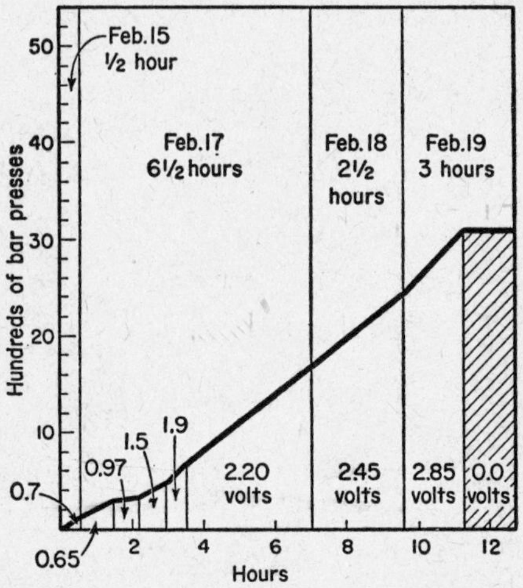

Fig. 5. Smoothed cumulative response curve for rat No. 32. Cumulative response totals are given along the ordinate, and hours along the abscissa. The steepness of the slope indicates the response rate. Stimulating voltages are given between black lines. Cross hatching indicates extinction.

three-quarters of its acquisition time responding. During the long period of extinction at the end of the day, there was very little responding, but *S* could be brought back to the lever quite quickly if a stimulus was delivered to show that the current had been turned on again.

DISCUSSION

It is clear that electrical stimulation in certain parts of the brain, particularly the septal area, produces acquisition and extinction curves which compare favorably with those produced by a conventional primary reward. With other electrode placements, the stimulation appears to be neutral or punishing.

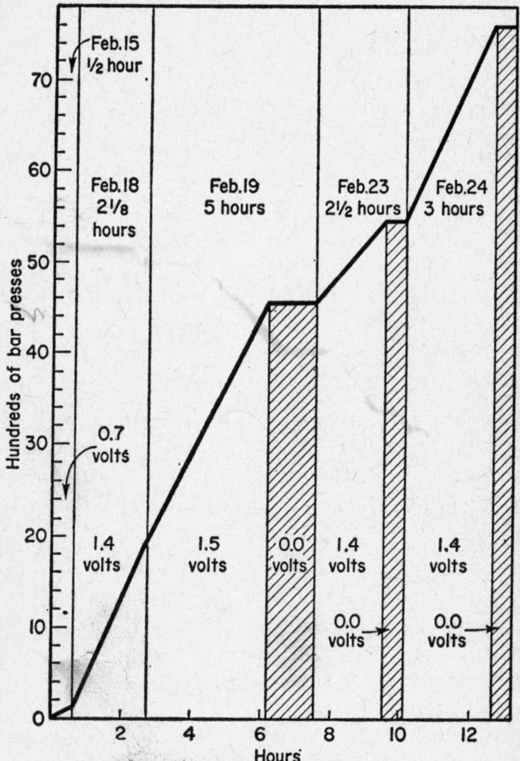

Fig. 6. Smoothed cumulative response curve for rat No. 34.

Because the rewarding effect has been produced maximally by electrical stimulation in the septal area, but also in lesser degrees in the mammillothalamic tract and cingulate cortex, we are led to speculate that a system of structures previously attributed to the rhinencephalon may provide the locus for the reward phenomenon. However, as localization studies which will map the whole brain with respect to the reward and punishment dimension are continuing, we will not discuss in detail the problem of locus. We will use the term "reinforcing structures" in further discussion as a general name for the septal area and other structures which produce the reward phenomenon.

To provide an adequate canvass of the possible explanations for the rewarding effect would require considerably more argument than could possibly fit within the confines of a research paper. We have decided, therefore, to rule out briefly the possibility that the implanta-

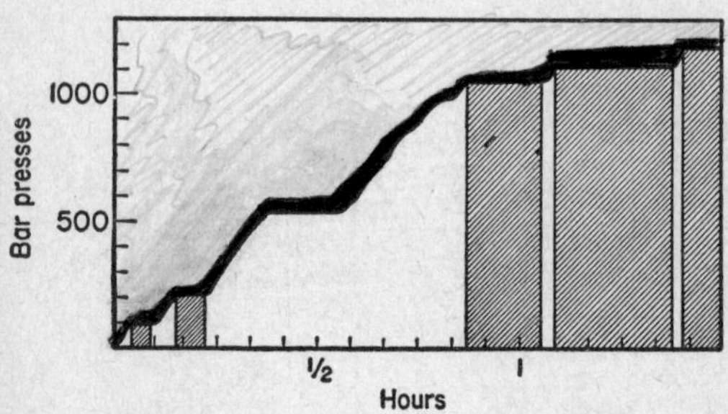

Fig. 7. Unsmoothed cumulative response curve showing about ¾ hr. extinction for rat No. A-5. Shading indicates extinction.

tion produces pain which is reduced by electrical stimulation of reinforcing structures, and to confine further discussion to suggestions of ways the phenomenon may provide a methodological basis for study of physiological mechanisms of reward.

The possibility that the implantation produces some painful "drive stimulus" which is alleviated by electrical stimulation of reinforcing structures does not comport with the facts which we have observed. If there were some chronic, painful drive state, it would be indicated by emotional signs in the animal's daily behavior. Our Ss, from the first day after the operation, are normally quiet, nonaggressive; they eat regularly, sleep regularly, gain

weight. There is no evidence in their behavior to support the postulation of chronic pain. Septal preparations which have lived healthy and normal lives for months after the operation have given excellent response rates.

As there is no evidence of a painful condition preceding the electrical stimulation, and as the animals are given free access to food and water at all times except while actually in the Skinner boxes, there is no explicitly manipulated drive to be reduced by electrical stimulation. Barring the possibility that stimulation of a reinforcing structure specifically inhibits the "residual drive" state of the animal, or the alternative possibility that the first electrical stimulus has noxious after-effects which are reduced by a second one, we have some evidence here for a primary rewarding effect which is not associated with the reduction of a primary drive state. It is perhaps fair in a discussion to report the "clinical impression" of the *E*s that the phenomenon represents strong pursuit of a positive stimulus rather than escape from some negative condition.

Should the latter interpretation prove correct, we have perhaps located a system within the brain whose peculiar function is to produce a rewarding effect on behavior. The location of such a system puts us in a position to collect information that may lead to a decision among conflicting theories of reward. By physiological studies, for example, we may find that the reinforcing structures act selectively on sensory or motor areas of the cortex. This would have relevance to current S-S versus S-R controversies (8, 9, 13, 16).

Similarly, extirpation studies may show whether reinforcing structures have primarily a quieting or an activating effect on behavior; this would be relevant to activation versus negative feedback theories of reward (6, 13, 15, 17). A recent study by Brady and Nauta (1) already suggests that the septal area is a quieting system, for its surgical removal produced an extremely active animal.

Such examples, we believe, make it reasonable to hope that the methodology reported here should have important consequences for physiological studies of mechanisms of reward.

SUMMARY

A preliminary study was made of rewarding effects produced by electrical stimulation of certain areas of the brain. In all cases rats were used and stimulation was by 60-cycle alternating current with voltages ranging from ½ to 5 v. Bipolar needle electrodes were permanently implanted at various points in the brain. Animals were tested in Skinner boxes where they could stimulate themselves by pressing a lever. They received no other reward than the electrical stimulus in the course of the experiments. The primary findings may be listed as follows: (*a*) There are numerous places in the lower centers of the brain where electrical stimulation is rewarding in the sense that the experimental animal will stimulate itself in these places frequently and regularly for long periods of time if permitted to do so. (*b*) It is possible to obtain these results from as far back as the tegmentum, and as far forward as the septal area; from as far down as the subthalamus, and as far up as the cingulate gyrus of the cortex. (*c*) There are also sites in the lower centers where the effect is just the opposite: animals do everything possible to avoid stimulation. And there are neutral sites: animals do nothing to obtain or to avoid stimulation. (*d*) The reward results are obtained more dependably with electrode placements in some areas than others, the septal area being the most dependable to date. (*e*) In septal area preparations, the control exercised over the animal's behavior by means of this reward is extreme, possibly exceeding that exercised by any other reward previously used in animal experimentation.

The possibility that the reward results depended on some chronic painful consequences of the implantation operation was ruled out on the evidence that no physiological or behavioral signs of such pain could be found. The phenomenon was discussed as possibly laying a methodological foundation for a physiological study of the mechanisms of reward.

REFERENCES

1. BRADY, J. V., & NAUTA, W. J. H. Subcortical mechanisms in emotional behavior: affective changes fol-

lowing septal forebrain lesions in the albino rat. *J. comp. physiol. Psychol.*, 1953, **46**, 339-346.
2. DELGADO, J. M. R. Permanent implantation of multilead electrodes in the brain. *Yale J. Biol. Med.*, 1952, **24**, 351-358.
3. DELGADO, J. M. R. Responses evoked in waking cat by electrical stimulation of motor cortex. *Amer. J. Physiol.*, 1952, **171**, 436-446.
4. DELGADO, J. M. R., & ANAND, B. K. Increase of food intake induced by electrical stimulation of the lateral hypothalamus. *Amer. J. Physiol.*, 1953, **172**, 162-168.
5. DELL, P. Correlations entre le système vegetatif et le système de la vie relation: mesencephale, diencephale, et cortex cerebral. *J. Physiol.* (Paris), 1952, **44**, 471-557.
6. DEUTSCH, J. A. A new type of behavior theory. *Brit. J. Psychol.*, 1953, **44**, 304-317.
7. GASTAUT, H. Correlations entre le système nerveux vegetatif et le système de la vie de relation dans le rhinencephale. *J. Physiol.* (Paris), 1952, **44**, 431-470.
8. HEBB, D. O. *The organizations of behavior.* New York: Wiley, 1949.
9. HULL, C. L. *Principles of behavior.* New York: D. Appleton-Century, 1943.
10. HUNTER, J., & JASPER, H. H. Effects of thalamic stimulation in unanaesthetized animals. *EEG clin. Neurophysiol.*, 1949, **1**, 305-324.
11. KRIEG, W. J. S. Accurate placement of minute lesions in the brain of the albino rat. *Quart. Bull., Northwestern Univer. Med. School,* 1946, **20**, 199-208.
12. MACLEAN, P. D., & DELGADO, J. M. R. Electrical and chemical stimulation of frontotemporal portion of limbic system in the waking animal. *EEG clin. Neurophysiol.*, 1953, **5**, 91-100.
13. OLDS, J. A neural model for sign-gestalt theory. *Psychol. Rev.*, 1954, **61**, 59-72.
14. ROSVOLD, H. E., & DELGADO, J. M. R. The effect on the behavior of monkeys of electrically stimulating or destroying small areas within the frontal lobes. *Amer. Psychologist,* 1953, **8**, 425-426. (Abstract)

15. SEWARD, J. P. Introduction to a theory of motivation in learning. *Psychol. Rev.*, 1952, **59**, 405-413.
16. SKINNER, B. F. *The behavior of organisms.* New York: D. Appleton-Century, 1938.
17. WIENER, N. *Cybernetics.* New York: Wiley, 1949.

14

Shortcomings of Food Consumption as a Measure of Hunger; Results from Other Behavioral Techniques

NEAL E. MILLER

Yale University

I have been tremendously impressed by the work so effectively reported at the Conference on which this monograph is based. It is interesting to note, however, that almost all of the studies referred to have used as their index of hunger a single technique, namely, the amount of food eaten. If one is interested in weight regulation, or the long-range balance between energy input and output, this method is an entirely appropriate measure. If one is interested in the broader problem of hunger as a drive, or in the complete mechanism of hunger and satiation, this measure has a number of limitations. It can profitably be supplemented by certain other behavioral techniques.

A little thought shows us that the amount of food eaten does not necessarily measure the maximum intensity of the hunger. For example, a persistent, or recurring, low level of hunger which keeps the subject nibbling would cause a large consumption of food, while an intense but rapidly satiated hunger would produce a smaller consumption. Furthermore, the total consumption probably depends on the balance between *two* factors: hunger and the motivation to stop eating.

The foregoing type of analysis is supported by a study by Miller, Bailey, and Stevenson[3] on rats with the hy-

---

This article originally appeared in the *Annals* of the New York Academy of Sciences, 1955, 63, pp. 141-143.

pothalamic lesions which cause obesity. On *ad lib.* feeding tests, these animals ate much *more* food than did normal controls. But a series of behavioral tests showed that they worked *less hard* for food and were *more easily* deterred from eating it. Therefore, we concluded that, under certain conditions, the hypothalamic animals can react to food deprivation with a less intense hunger, even though they eat more on an *ad lib.* diet.*

I shall briefly illustrate two of the behavioral measures which we have found useful in this and other studies. The one is the rate of bar pressing aperiodically reinforced by food as originally developed by Skinner[6] at Harvard and extensively used in our laboratory at Yale. First, hungry animals are trained to press a bar which always immediately delivers a small pellet of food into a little dish below. Then the mechanism is set so that pressing the bar will deliver food only at certain unpredictable intervals. The animals continue working much like a gambler who operates a slot machine in the hope of hitting the jackpot. The rate at which they work seems to be a good measure of the strength of hunger. Furthermore, since the animals get only tiny bits of food infrequently, relatively long tests can be made without appreciably satiating hunger.

The other measure involves pitting the aversion produced by quinine against appetite. Animals are presented with a series of tiny samples of food, each of which is adulterated by an increasing proportion of quinine. As might be expected, the hungrier animals progress farther up the series into the higher concentrations of quinine. In our study of the hypothalamic animals, both the bar pressing and the quinine showed the same reduction in hunger which contrasted with the increase in the *ad lib.* consumption of a high-fat diet.

A somewhat similar discrepancy between the consummatory and the other two behavioral measures appears in studying the effects of different durations of food deprivation. We have compared four techniques under exactly the same conditions. The amount of food which

* Under somewhat different conditions, which are not yet well understood by us, the rats with hypothalamic lesions can not only eat more but also work harder for food.

the rats ate immediately after various periods of deprivation increased rapidly during the first 6 hours and reached a maximum somewhere in the neighborhood of 30 hours, after which it tended to fall off. The total excursion of stomach contractions (recorded from a balloon on the end of a chronically implanted plastic fistula) increased rapidly during the first six hours, after which it tended to level off. But our other two measures, the rate of bar pressing and the amount of quinine required to stop eating, continued to increase with food deprivation throughout the 54 hours measured. In some of our other experiments, the rate of bar pressing has continued to *increase* for at least 4 days, while the amount of food consumed has continued to *decrease* after 24 hours. Thus, at the higher levels, the amount of food consumed does not seem to be a good measure of hunger. It seems to be limited by the volume of the stomach, or the capacity of the organism to deal with the food. Furthermore, this limit decreases during more extreme deprivation.

Under other circumstances, the consummatory and the performance measures may agree. The studies made in our laboratory of the role of oral-pharyngeal factors are good examples.* Kohn[2] found that the rate of bar pressing aperiodically reinforced by food was relatively unaffected by an immediately preceding injection of 14 cc. of isotonic saline directly into the stomach via chronic plastic fistula. But 14 cc. of milk injected directly into the stomach produced a marked reduction in the rate of bar pressing, and the same amount of milk drunk normally by mouth produced an even greater reduction. Berkun, Kessen, and Miller[1] secured exactly similar results when the amount of milk drunk was used as a test. Furthermore, Miller and Kessen[4] found that milk injected directly into the stomach served as a reward for learning a simple T-maze, but that milk taken normally by mouth served as a stronger reward to produce more rapid learning.

As a supplement to the chronic fistula technique, we have used saccharin, a sweet tasting but nonnutritive sub-

* Supported in part by a research grant, M647, from the National Institute of Mental Health, of the National Institutes of Health, United States Public Health Service.

stance, to test for oral-pharyngeal effects. As a control, we have used an equal volume of a saline solution matched for sodium content with the sodium saccharide. In one series of experiments, this control solution was administered by mouth. So that they would drink it, the rats were thirsty as well as hungry. Tests showed that the saline and saccharin solutions were equally effective in reducing thirst, but differed in their short-range effects on hunger. Compared with the control, prefeeding with saccharin solution reduced both the subsequent consumption of that solution and the rate of bar pressing reinforced by saccharin. It also reduced the immediately succeeding consumption of dextrose, milk, lab chow, or fat. The effects of saccharin were less, however, than those of an equally preferred solution of dextrose. This reduction seemed to be due to the fact that dextrose had both an oral-pharyngeal and a gastrointestinal effect, while saccharin had only the former. In contrast with the results on nutritive substances, saccharin administered via stomach fistula had no effect; only when taken by mouth did it reduce subsequent consumption or performance.

In conclusion, I should like to illustrate how yet another behavioral technique has been used to demonstrate a qualitative difference between two otherwise similar effects. We have studied the effects of stomach distention by using rats with two plastic fistulas chronically implanted into their stomachs. On the end of one of these fistulas was a rubber balloon. We compared the effect of injecting milk via fistula into the stomach with that of injecting an equal volume of a saline solution of equal specific gravity into the balloon in the stomach. Both procedures reduced the rate at which rats would work at pressing a bar to get food. The effects of the milk were slightly, but statistically reliably, greater. When studied by this technique, the effects of stomach distention by balloon and by milk were qualitatively similar, and only slightly different quantitatively. In other experiments[5] we used a learning technique. Hungry rats were given trials in a simple T-maze. If they chose a given side (for example, turned to the right), one group had milk injected via fistula directly into their stomachs, and the other group had an equal volume of saline injected into their stomach balloons. The rats whose stomachs were distended by milk learned to *choose* that side, but the rats whose stomachs were distended by the balloon learned to *avoid* that side. We can conclude that two qualitatively different factors must be involved. One of these factors might be a reduction in the strength of the hunger drive, which should be rewarding, and the other might be the induction of some conflicting motivation, such as nausea, which should be punishing. In any event, it is clear that the rewarding effects were dominant when the stomach was distended by milk and the punishing ones were dominant when it was distended by the balloon. The two treatments produced qualitatively different effects.

REFERENCES

1. BERKUN, M. M., M. L. KESSEN & N. E. MILLER. 1952. "Hunger-reducing effects of food by stomach fistula versus food by mouth measured by a consummatory response." *J. Comp. Physiol. Psychol.* 45: 550-554.
2. KOHN, M. 1951. "Satiation of hunger from food injected directly into the stomach versus food ingested by mouth." *J. Comp. Physiol. Psychol.* 44: 412-422.
3. MILLER, N. E., C. J. BAILEY & J. A. F. STEVENSON. 1950. "Decreased 'hunger' but increased food intake resulting from hypothalamic lesions." *Science.* 112: 256-259.
4. MILLER, N. E. & M. L. KESSEN. 1952. "Reward effects of food via stomach fistula compared with those of food via mouth." *J. Comp. Physiol. Psychol.* 45: 555-564.
5. MILLER, N. E. & M. L. KESSEN. 1954. "Is distention of the stomach via balloon rewarding or punishing?" *Am. Psychol.* 99: 430-431.
6. SKINNER, B. F. 1938. *The Behavior of Organisms.* Appleton-Century. New York, N.Y.

Part V

15

Comments on Selected Controversial Issues

NEAL E. MILLER

THE NATURE OF REINFORCEMENT

It seems to be a fact that some stimulus situations are much more effective than others in determining whether or not the responses that lead to them will be learned and performed. Thus, all theorists are forced to assign the empirical law of effect some role in their theories. A consistent application of the empirical law of effect would result in a long list of stimulus situations that can serve as rewards and of those that are relatively neutral. In practice, most experimenters limit themselves to relatively few situations which are known to function as effective rewards.

The drive-stimulus-reduction hypothesis. Since a catalogue of rewards is so cumbersome, some theorists have looked for a simple general principle, or principles, that will allow them to determine whether an event should be listed as a reward or not. One attempt at such a principle is the drive-reduction hypothesis of reinforcement.

It is well known that turning off a strong motivational stimulus, such as an electric shock, will serve as a reward to reinforce whatever response the animal was making just before he escaped from the shock. It is also known

---

This portion of Miller's review of the contemporary state of S-R theory is directly concerned with the theme of this volume. As such it makes an excellent summary statement. Note his remarks on the utility of the drive-stimulus-reduction hypothesis. (Reprinted by permission from *Psychology: A Study of a Science,* Vol. 2, edited by Sigmund Koch. Copyright, 1959. McGraw-Hill Book Co., Inc.)

that food will serve as a reward for a hungry animal, and that this same food, if given in sufficient quantities, will reduce the strength of the hunger drive. The drive-reduction hypothesis attempts to abstract a common element from observations of this kind. In its weak form, it states that the sudden reduction in the strength of any strong motivational stimulus always serves as a reward, or in other words, is a *sufficient* condition for reinforcement. In its strong form, it states that all reward is produced in this way, or in other words, that drive reduction is not only a sufficient but also the *necessary* condition for reinforcement.

By defining drives as strong stimuli, I have sharpened the hypothesis into the assumption that it is the sudden reduction in the strength of intense stimulation that serves as a reinforcement.

Not completely committed to drive-stimulus-reduction hypothesis. Although I believe that the foregoing hypothesis has a considerably less than 50 per cent chance of being correct, especially in its strong form, I do believe it is better at the present moment than any other single hypothesis. Therefore, I feel that it is worthwhile to try out applying it consistently, if only to highlight the obstacles and infuriate others into devising superior hypotheses and the experimental programs to support them.

When one systematically explores a given hypothesis and points out the weaknesses of various theoretical and experimental attacks on this hypothesis, however, it is difficult to avoid the reputation (and after that, the fact) of being emotionally fixated on the hypothesis. Furthermore, the very controversial nature of the drive-stimulus-reduction hypothesis makes it conspicuous, so that it seems to be the cornerstone of one's whole theoretical thinking.

Let me try to destroy both illusions. The stimulus-reduction hypothesis of reinforcement could be discarded without having an appreciable effect on the rest of my theoretical formulations. I take this occasion to urge attempts to formulate and rigorously test competing hypotheses, and time permitting, may even join in that activity myself. However unsatisfactory, the drive-reduction hypothesis is not likely to be abandoned as long as it is the best thing of its kind that we have. The decisive way to kill it is with a superior alternative.

Various possible bases for correlation between reinforcement and satiation. Let us start out with the original observation that there seems to be a correlation between the operations of satiation and those of reinforcement. This is not surprising because animals that are not rewarded by substances that reduce their drives are likely to come from a long line of extinct ancestors. Furthermore, the process could also work the other way—individuals that do not eventually become satiated on a given form of pleasure may starve to death while enjoying the thrill of tickling themselves.

We should remember that a correlation does not necessarily indicate a direct causal relationship. The drive reduction could produce the reinforcement, the reinforcement could produce the drive reduction, or natural selection could have built a correlation into the organism that did not involve any direct causal relationship. For example, an increase in pleasure could be the true basis for reinforcement and animals could have evolved by natural selection so that in general only nutritious substances taste good and the pleasantness of these is some function of the strength of hunger.

Sample studies illustrating fruitfulness of hypothesis. If natural selection has produced a spurious correlation, we would expect this correlation to be more likely to disappear if we manipulated drives in unusual ways which have not been encountered in natural selection. On the other hand, if it is a true causal relationship, it should survive these unusual manipulations.

In order to test the drive-reduction hypothesis in this way, and also to learn more about the mechanism of drives, I have been involved in a series of experiments which have attempted to induce and reduce drives in unusual ways. These experiments have shown that food injected via a plastic fistula directly into the stomach of a rat promptly reduces hunger as measured either by the amount of food subsequently eaten or by the rate at which the animals will work at pressing a bar to secure food on a variable-interval schedule of reinforcement. But food taken normally by mouth has a greater effect on both of these two measures. Similar results have been secured for thirst, which has also been induced by injecting hypertonic saline into the ventricles of the brain and reduced by injecting water. In short, there seem to be a number of mechanisms—located in the mouth, stomach, and brain—for regulating drive.

Furthermore, exactly as the drive-reduction hypothesis would predict from the foregoing facts, food injected directly into the stomach will serve as a reward to cause rats to choose the correct side of a T maze, but food taken normally by mouth will serve as a stronger reward to produce more rapid learning. The rewarding effect of food injected directly into the stomach would not be expected from hypotheses that used either the pleasant taste or the consummatory response as the sole basis of reinforcement. Conversely, the saccharine solution which Sheffield and Roby proved was a reward for hungry animals has been found by us to reduce hunger.

Effects of electrical stimulation of the brain. Another series of studies has demonstrated the possibilities of motivating learning and performance by direct electrical stimulation of the brain. In connection with these studies, I have discussed the implications for theories of reinforcement of the reward effect discovered by Olds and Milner and have shown how the drive-stimulus-reduction hypothesis can suggest significant new studies of central motivation and reward—studies which ultimately may lead to a superior hypothesis. A summary of my recent physiological studies of motivation has been published elsewhere.

Campbell's psychophysical studies. The hypothesis that drives are strong stimuli and that sudden reductions in them produce reinforcement, has further demonstrated its usefulness by starting Byron Campbell on a series of studies which extend the psychophysical tradition to a new area by quantitatively studying the rewarding effects of sudden reductions in the strength of strong stimuli. Electric shocks and loud sounds have been used in these studies which show that, when the stimulation is reduced to zero, stronger initial strengths of stimulation produce greater learning and performance. But when the motivation is not reduced to zero, a given absolute amount of reduction is less effective the higher the initial level. Within the middle ranges, equal reinforcing effects seem to be produced by equal ratios of reduction, a relationship like Weber's law, which breaks down at the extremes. Thus, what might be described as a "reinforcement threshold" seems to show the same general type of curve as does the psychophysical threshold for a just noticeable difference, although much larger changes are required to produce a reinforcing effect.

Relationship of drive to learning. A stimulus-response analysis can clarify some of the apparent confusion concerning the relationship of drive to learning. In the practical teaching situation, everyone knows that poorly motivated students do not learn. This is chiefly because they do not expose themselves to the proper cues or perform the correct responses, for example, open their books and study. But most experiments on this topic have concerned themselves with a somewhat different problem: the relationship of drive to reinforcement. Therefore, they have tried to control the factors of exposure to cues and number of responses by giving both groups the same number of trials in very simple situations. One must be careful in generalizing from this kind of experiment to the practical situation; a film of mine yields a better analogy.

When the drive is promptly reduced to zero after the correct response, there is a perfect correlation between the strength of drive and the amount of drive reduction. Thus, according to the stimulus-reduction hypothesis, stronger drives should produce more reinforcement and better learning. These conditions are met in most experiments on escape learning and eyelid conditioning. The results of such experiments agree with the theory.[8]

In the work of Campbell and his collaborators, we have just seen that when the drive stimulus is reduced a *constant absolute value,* the amount of reinforcement follows the same Weber's law principle as other stimuli; it is less at the higher levels of drive. Under these circum-

[8] It should be noted, however, that all such experiments have involved noxious stimuli so that one might claim that the positive results were produced by a learned drive, such as fear, which persisted from training to testing.

stances, the intense-stimulus-reduction hypothesis would not expect a positive relationship between the strength of drive and amount of learning.

In experiments in which the correct response is reinforced by pellets of food or sips of water, it is obvious that, at the extreme low end of the continuum, there will be little possibility of drive reduction if there is almost no drive present. And indeed, experiments on so-called latent learning seem to agree that extremely low drives (whether all relevant primary and secondary drives are zero is controversial) seem to produce less learning than does higher drive.

When we start comparing moderate drives with strong ones, however, we simply do not know what the relationship is between the strength of drive and the *relative* amount of drive reduction produced by a single pellet of food or sip of water. Therefore, it should not be too surprising that the results of such experiments are confusing. Even if the the animal were fed to satiation at the end of a trial, the total amount of drive reduction would be confounded with considerable delay. Perhaps techniques for manipulating hunger and thirst by electrical stimulation of the brain (or measuring them by central recording) will develop to the point where we can conduct decisive experiments on such drives.

Spence has clearly pointed out and documented an additional source of possible confusion, namely, that whenever an incorrect response is dominant at the beginning of learning, Hull's principle that drive multiplies the strength of habits predicts that increases in drive will increase its excitatory potential more than that of the subdominant correct responses. To this and other excellent points that he makes, I would add only that one must consider (1) possible innate responses to different strengths of drive, and (2) the possibility that rates and amplitudes are specific responses as would be expected from a micromolar analysis of the type expounded by Logan.

Large areas in which lack of suitable measures makes hypothesis inapplicable. In experiments using extremely strong stimuli, such as electric shocks, intense lights, or sounds that are under external control, the stimulus-reduction hypothesis clearly applies and is routinely verified. But perhaps the most damning thing that can be said about this hypothesis is that there are so many situations in which, with our present techniques, we cannot tell for certain whether the net effect of a given experimental operation is to produce an increase or a decrease in the motivating stimulus. Although such limitations are not unique to this hypothesis, a clear-cut possibility of disproof would be preferable to the present ambiguity. For example, if the change from complete darkness to weak illumination is reinforcing, it can be argued that the small increase in visual stimulation is more than overbalanced by a reduction in boredom or fear. Similarly, it can be argued either that tiny pellets of food produce brief reductions in drive, or that they do not appreciably reduce hunger and may even whet the animal's appetite. Guthrie can argue that a boy banging on a drum is seeking stimulation and Harlow can say the same concerning the curiosity of his monkeys. On the other hand, a plausible case can be made that both boy and monkey are escaping from the intolerable tension of boredom. Such ambiguities have motivated me to the program of research aimed at trying to learn more about the mechanisms of drive induction and reduction. Perhaps there are physiological ways of securing independent measures of at least certain drives, or behavioral techniques for trying to extend the correlation between satiation and reinforcement to other drives such as curiosity.

Alternative hypotheses. Guthrie's version of the pure contiguity hypothesis is enormously appealing because of its simplicity and because it would be relatively easy to imagine a physiological mechanism that worked in this way. I have been unable to see, however, why it should not predict that a thoroughly learned response to a momentary stimulus will never extinguish. After a given response is learned to the point where it regularly is the first and last response to that stimulus, should not more and more of the atypical members of the population of cues be conditioned to the response so that it would become progressively more certain to occur?

There is also the problem of why the stimulus-change produced by the *onset* of a painful stimulus does not protect preceding responses from retroactive inhibition. One might modify Guthrie's hypothesis to avoid these difficulties by assuming that only the termination of a stimulus (and *not* changes produced by adding new cues) functions to protect responses from retroactive inhibition, and that such protection is proportional to the number of cue elements that are removed. Then, the effect of terminating a weak stimulus would be negligible because the change in the total population of cue elements would be so small, but the termination of a strong stimulus would be more effective because many more cue elements would be removed. With such modifications, Guthrie's application of the contiguity hypothesis would become functionally very similar to the hypothesis that reinforcement is produced by the prompt reduction in a strong stimulus.

Various two-factor theories have considerable attractiveness. It is easy to imagine a simple contiguity mechanism being evolved at an early stage and then supplemented with some sort of booster effect from reward or the escape from punishment. Indeed, it is quite possible that careful research on primitive organisms, or on more complex ones primitivized by removing higher segments of the brain, would show that it is possible for them to learn several responses by simple conditioning but not to select among them by trial and error, even when the proper conditions for trial and error learning are realized.

Actually, the shift from a single factor to a multifactor theory need not be very disruptive to the general features of such miniature systems as I have proposed as long as most of the laws—gradient of reinforcement, stimulus generalization, experimental extinction, spontaneous recovery, etc.—remain the same as before. These laws seem to be the same for classically conditioned autonomic responses as well as for trial-and-error somatic responses reinforced by either escape from electric shock or rewarding a hungry animal with food.

To use a simple analogy, to change the lighting in an apartment house from electricity to gas, would be a major undertaking because the two sources of energy follow completely different laws, and thus would require changes such as those from wires to pipes. A change from a-c to d-c current would involve relatively minor alterations, since these two types of current have relatively similar functional properties. A shift from alternating current delivered by a private company to alternating current delivered by a municipal one would involve only a small change in the connections to the basement (which, indeed, would be highly significant to those who sell the current from different sources), but there would be no changes in the wiring and appliances throughout the apartment house since the current from these two sources follows identical laws.

Proponents of multiple-factor theories of learning can attract more serious attention if they can rigorously specify different laws associated with supposedly different types of learning.

Cognitive theories. S-R theorists are confronted with the problem of explaining man's obviously intelligent behavior; cognitive theorists are confronted with the problem of explaining obvious stupidity. Although recognizing that much of man's behavior involves cognitions, I have preferred the strategy of trying to explain such behavior as the outgrowth of simpler, noncognitive mechanisms. It is hard for me to conceive of cognitive insight as the sole means of acquiring maladaptive neurotic symptoms or those many motor skills that seem to be almost entirely unconscious.

One obvious alternative taken by many cognitive theorists is to assume different levels of learning—a lower S-R one to explain stupid behavior and a higher cognitive one to explain intelligent behavior. This may turn out to be the most parsimonious explanation possible, but the theorist will have to be careful to specify under what conditions both occur or else he will be limited to *post hoc* explanations. Another alternative is to adopt the general pattern of Tolman's theory—using association as the basic element of learning, and the empirical law of effect as the mechanism of activation—but stating the laws in terms of automatic processes. Spence's theory is tending in this direction. Variations of this general pattern certainly should be rigorously explored. But one must be careful that the theory does not predict that, if rats or earthworms show any learning with motivation and reward, they should show approximately as good latent learning.

NEW TRAILS FOR RESEARCH ON MOTIVATION[9]

We are still a long way from a satisfactory understanding of motivation. To take a simple example, much of our human social behavior is overdetermined by many different sources of drive and reinforcement. Thus, money is the focus of many needs; its possession the means to many rewards. But our experimental literature has scarcely started to tackle the problems of how different sources of drive and reward summate positively or negatively in the learning and maintenance of a given habit.

Learned elicitation vs. learned channeling. Most of the motivation of adult human social behavior is either acquired by or profoundly modified by learning. I have called such motivations *learnable drives and rewards* to emphasize the fact that the basic physiological mechanism is probably innate, although the arousal or reduction in response to specific cues is a product of learning [64]. In the case of fear, it seems possible for part of the response innately elicited by pain (loud sounds and perhaps a considerable variety of other situations) to be conditioned to new cues so that it can be elicited in the complete absence of any obvious, relevant primary drive. Let us call this *learned elicitation.*

I have assumed that the elicitation of a number of social drives might be learned in the same way as fear, for example, as a result of thousands of instances in which feeding and other sources of infant gratification are associated with the appearance of an approving parent. However, I have repeatedly failed to establish experimentally any appreciable learned elicitation of drive on the basis of primary drives such as hunger or thirst.[10]

[9] Throughout this section I frequently use the term motivation to include the effects of both drive and reward, using the latter terms if I want to distinguish the two effects.

[10] It is conceivable that this failure is due to the fact that these drives are aroused so slowly that one is always dealing with delayed, or even backward, conditioning. That is one of

Although this failure has not caused me to abandon completely the attempt to apply the fear-elicitation paradigm to appetitive drives, it has caused me to shift the emphasis in a new direction. As pointed out earlier, even the primary drives themselves may be profoundly modified by learning, so that hunger becomes the desire for a particular kind of food prepared according to culturally determined standards of what is appetizing. Thus, one must learn to like snails or oysters. But the elicitation of the appetite for such foods never becomes completely independent of hunger, since even these delicacies have little appeal after complete satiation by a Thanksgiving dinner. Furthermore, although the taste for snails and other exotic foods is learned, it is continually reinforced by eating them when hungry. Therefore, one does not need to worry about the problem of experimental extinction vs. functional autonomy.

It should be noted, however, that hunger probably can be channeled only to certain categories of objects, namely, foods. I venture that it would be much more difficult to develop and maintain an appetite for sawdust. Are there other drives that permit more latitude in channeling? What are the defining characteristics of their potential goal objects?

The desire for a specific kind of food may be called *learned channeling of drive*. It may be contrasted with the fear of a previously neutral cue which we have just described as learned elicitation of drive.

The foregoing two examples—channeling of hunger and elicitation of fear—may not be completely different, but represent the extremes of a continuum. An intermediate case could occur if there is a latent fear of some type of situation which can be further strengthened by learning. Or there might be an innate tendency to fear some general class of situations which can be made more specific by learning. Furthermore, we might find that the

---

the reasons why I have been interested in exploring possibilities of eliciting drives rapidly by techniques such as electrical or chemical stimulation of the brain. On the other hand, it may be that such failures are due to the absence of any mechanism for a response-produced drive like the one involved in fear.

reaction to a conditioned fear stimulus would vary with the general level of anxiety of the subject and be influenced by physiological factors such as endocrine changes.

Can rewards for one drive channel a different one? Another possibility is that reinforcement by the goal objects of a given drive may help to determine the direction in which a second one is channeled.[11] If such channeling occurs, it might easily be mistaken for the establishment of learned elicitation, and/or secondary reinforcement that became independent of the first drive.

A possible illustration of such a channeled drive is the Freudian hypothesis that sex begins as a dependent drive (*Anlehnungstriebe*), so that a young man's eventual object choice may be determined by earlier rewards in the nursing situation under the primary drive of hunger. If this were the case, it is clear that the young man's attraction to his bride might continue to be reinforced by adult sexual (and other) gratifications even though he discovered that she could not cook.

To take a simpler example, Scott has observed that two bottle-fed sheep showed no tendency whatsoever to follow the rest of the herd whereas several thousand normally nursed controls all showed strong gregarious tendencies. This observation suggests that gregariousness in sheep may be influenced by learning during the nursing situation. But some special innate susceptibility or additional source of motivation must be involved since not all mammals are as gregarious as sheep.

Similarly, a variety of obvious rewards, such as feeding, determine a dog's attachment to a particular master or family. This attachment may be strong enough to motivate the dog to learn to respond to various cues by being ready to leap into the car so that he will not be left behind. But equally well-treated cats usually do not acquire a similar motivation. Such observations raise the possibility that, as part of the pattern of hunting in packs, evolu-

[11] I use the more general phrase "reinforcement by goal objects" to emphasize the fact that this hypothesis is not necessarily tied to the drive-stimulus-reduction hypothesis of reinforcement.

tion has produced in dogs some special motivational mechanism that can be channeled either to the pack or to the adoptive human family.

The "imprinting" of ducks to follow people and other objects may be an extreme example of channeling. We have already suggested that this "motivation to follow" probably could be used as a drive for the trial-and-error learning of whatever response produced the release that permitted the baby duck to follow its leader. But the original behavior of the newly hatched duck in the absence of any suitable moving objects to follow suggests some strong original motivation, perhaps fear. Could this motivation also be studied? Would its reduction by a suitable object prove to be the source of reinforcement for the original imprinting? What role is played by feeding and other reinforcements which often are confounded with "imprinting"?

It is possible that the type of behavior which we have described as channeling is nothing more than an array of specific habits. Certainly the line between (or blending of) habit and motivation needs clarification as Brown has ably argued.

What I would like to point out is that such habits seem to have many of the functional properties of drives. Oysters for people, or novel foods for rats, do not function as effective rewards until the subject has learned to eat them. How much of this is a function of mere delay in seizing and swallowing? I venture that at least some of the effect may be due to the elimination of aversions by counterconditioning and the acquisition of secondary reinforcement.

Furthermore, the aroma, sight, or even description of a particular delicacy seems to produce a considerable increase in the motivation of a moderately hungry person. I venture that, under appropriate circumstances, it would also facilitate the trial-and-error learning and performance of any response that circumvented a block to the direct approach to the incentive. Furthermore, Tinklepaugh's observations on monkeys and my own incidental observations of people suggest that, once a learned strong anticipatory goal response for a particular food is aroused, other foods may be less effective as rewards. Again the factor of delay in consumption needs to be controlled.

Finally, we need to know the laws governing the ways in which motivation can be channeled and/or elicited by new cues. For example, what conditions can inhibit the development of intellectual curiosity in children and what conditions can enhance it? For that matter, what conditions can arrest, strengthen, or channel the curiosity of a cat?

Throughout the preceding discussion we have raised a number of theoretical possibilities. Although the animal examples cited should readily lend themselves to precise experimental analysis, such work has not been done, so that our discussion has had to be highly speculative; many different theoretical possibilities are open.

What drives may be elicited or channeled by learning? Since the conditions of social and individual learning are complex and variable, we will expect learnable drives to exist in a baffling variety of combinations in response to a baffling variety of cues. Thus, any standard list of socially learned motives will only be as simple and as stable as the conditions of learning involved. This may explain the baffling variety of such lists.

One might go on to ask, however, what kind of different physiological mechanisms may underlie learnable drives? It seems plausible that fear might be the underlying mechanism in a number of instances that seem different because different conditions of training have caused different categories of cues to arouse the fear, and other specific categories of cues to serve as the goals because they, respectively, reduce these specific fears. Thus, it is interesting to note that we speak of the fear of failure, the fear of disapproval, the fear of losing money, status, or love.

Similarly, Freudian theory presupposes that sex underlies a large number of superficially different motives.

Do certain social motives, such as curiosity, gregariousness, and jealousy, all have a common mechanism, or does each have distinctive ones? Can such motives be elicited, channeled, or both? If they are channeled, what are the characteristics defining potential goals? We have scarcely made a beginning toward answering some of these questions. If we knew more about some of these other sources of motivation, we might not be so strongly tempted to place such a heavy theoretical burden on fear. We must solve such problems before we can begin to understand the wonderfully complex web of human social motivation.

Need to study new types of drive; one way to do it. Most of the basic research on motivation to date has been confined to an extremely limited number of so-called primary drives such as hunger, thirst, sex, and pain. There is a great need to study new types of motivation in the laboratory. Our present list of experimentally studied motives is far too short. A promising break away from our old limitations has been made with studies of fear and more recent studies of "curosity" and "activity." We need to extrapolate this new trend.

A *new view of fear.* The old view of fear as an emotion was inferior in that it stressed innate and disrupting effects of fear and did not even give a clear picture of how these were achieved. The newer and much more powerful understanding is (a) that fear is a drive, like hunger or thirst, which may motivate either adaptive or maladaptive behavior, and (b) that a sudden reduction in the strength of fear serves as a reward to reinforce immediately preceding responses.

The point of departure for this new understanding of fear was Mowrer's trenchant stimulus-response analysis of Freud's insightful paper on the problem of anxiety. Mowrer's pioneering work led me to set up an experimental demonstration that fear has a crucial functional property of drive in that it can motivate the trial-and-error learning and performance of whatever response is followed by a sudden reduction in the strength of fear. I believe that this same experimental paradigm that I applied to fear can be used to study many other sources of motivation.

In my experiment on fear, albino rats were placed in a simple apparatus consisting of two compartments separated by a door. One was white with a grid as a floor; the other was black without a grid. Before training, the animals showed no marked preference for either compartment. Then, they were given a number of trials during which they received electric shock in the white compartment and escaped into the black compartment through the open door. After this training, the animals would run out of the white compartment, even if no shock was on the grid.

Then, during additional trials without further shocks came the critical test to demonstrate that the rats' running was not the mere persistence of a habit, but also had the crucial property of a drive, namely that it could motivate, and its reduction reinforce, the learning of a *new* habit. The door, previously always open, was closed. The only way that it could be opened was by rotating, by a fraction of a turn, a little wheel which was above the door. Under these conditions, the rats exhibited trial-and-error behavior and gradually learned to escape from the white compartment by promptly rotating the wheel.

When the conditions were changed, so that only pressing a bar would open the door, wheel turning extinguished and a second, new habit (bar pressing) was learned. Thus, the fear, presumably established by the shocks in the white compartment, was shown to have the same functional properties as a drive such as pain in that it could motivate the trial-and-error performance of response and its reduction could reinforce the immediately preceding response.

This new view that fear is a drive and that fear-reduction is a reinforcement has many consequences. These have been developed in the course of studies in which I have been involved—investigations of behavior in combat, and an analysis of neurosis and psychotherapy. In going beyond the experimental studies of animals in vital fear situations, I have chosen to look for "naturally" occurring situations where people were confronted with vital dangers, rather than bringing subjects into the relatively safe laboratory and in effect merely saying "boo!" to them.[12] I shall have space to hint at only a few of the main points gleaned from such studies. Many

[12] My work in the Air Force during World War II convinced me of the difficulties of devising situations that would really frighten eager young aviation cadets without terrifying generals and congressmen.

of the ideas emerged from collaboration with John Dollard.

As soon as fear is thought of as a drive, one notices that it can motivate desirable behavior, such as being alert and resourceful, driving slowly, looking for the source of danger and planning ways to minimize it—for example, buying insurance. Of course, fear can also motivate undesirable behavior such as cowardly running and hiding, cheating, and lying. The most important thing, then is *not how afraid a man is but what fear motivates him to do.*

Since a sudden reduction in the intensity of fear serves as a reward to strengthen responses, a frightened person will learn those responses he is making when his fear is reduced. If he eventually escapes from the fear by brave, adaptive behavior, he should learn to become more courageous and resourceful; if he temporarily reduces fear by cowardly and maladaptive behavior, he should learn to become more craven. If neurotic symptoms reduce fear, they will be learned. Other symptoms, such as ulcers, may be part of the direct physiological reaction to fear.

One way of reducing fear is to turn away from, suppress, or repress the fear-arousing stimuli. When mild fears are reduced in this way, the subject learns to avoid unpleasant topics; when intense fears are involved, complete repression may be reinforced. It is obvious that avoiding looking at and thinking about possible sources of danger may actually increase the probability of disaster or decrease the possibility of making the discrimination that no significant danger exists. Furthermore, anyone who wants to use fear as a motivation must effectively emphasize the proper escapes from fear or run the danger of having his subjects find their own escape by avoiding him and forgetting his message. In using fear as a drive it is important to remember that *the escape from fear is what reinforces learned behavior.*

Many additional practical points come out of the naturalistic study of fear, for example, the importance of knowing exactly what to expect or planning and knowing what to do to minimize the danger, of concentrating on the task at hand, of breaking seemingly impossible tasks into manageable steps and concentrating on the successful performance of each step, the value of reassurance from the group or self-administered reassurance, the effectiveness of strong positive motivation and of rewards (counterconditioning) for nonfearful behavior. Additional discussion more oriented toward theory and experiment will be found in Miller.

Curiosity. In the course of a fruitless search for a learned drive based on hunger, Myers and Miller have applied to curiosity the same apparatus and theoretical paradigm that had been used in the study of fear. Curiosity had previously been brought into the laboratory from somewhat different points of view by the ingenious work done by Berlyne, Harlow, and Montgomery. In addition to applying the same operations used in the study of fear, Myers and I suggested the importance of determining whether a new drive, such as curiosity, shows the same pattern of deprivation-reinforcement-satiation as previously studied drives such as hunger. In other words, is there a correlation between the operations of reinforcement and satiation, so that an event which increases the *subsequent* performance of a response when administered immediately after that response is also found to tend to decrease the performance of responses motivated by that drive when it is administered in sufficient amount immediately before testing those responses? [13]

Finally, Kagan and Berkun have used the same general paradigm for studying "activity drive" and Zimbardo and Miller have used it as the point of departure for studying the effect of hunger on curiosity.

Drive elicited by perceptual mechanism? The general approach can be further illustrated by another experiment. In an attempt to bridge the gap between gestalt

[13] It should be noted that one can imagine special conditions under which the drive-stimulus-reduction hypothesis would not demand quite the same pattern as hunger seems to exhibit. Suppose pressing a bar turned off a shock which was almost immediately turned back on. There would be a correlation between the operations of reinforcement and satiation, but the period of "satiation" might be so brief that it easily could be missed. Furthermore, longer periods of "deprivation" might not produce greater amounts of recovery from "satiation."

theory, perceptual learning, and S-R theory, I wondered whether the vector toward a good gestalt had the properties of a drive. If it did, one might expect animals exposed to a bad gestalt to learn by trial and error a simple response that would cause it to change to a better one. The "bad gestalt" of a series of broken lines was projected in front of pigeons. Pecking on a response key caused this to change to the "good gestalt" of unbroken lines. For a control group, the same response caused a pattern of straight lines to change to one of broken lines.

To circumvent certain practical difficulties, we started with trained birds, tried to measure any reinforcing effect by a difference in resistance to extinction, and introduced a number of controls for possible stimulus generalization between the situations of training and of extinction.

The difference, although in the right direction, was relatively small and unreliable. Perhaps a tendency toward a good gestalt cannot function as a drive, or perhaps we used a technique that elicited it only weakly. But the experiment illustrates how the method can be applied.

With sufficiently ingenious apparatus, the same general method could be used to determine whether or not motivational effects are produced by sensory blurring, perceptual distortions, or the disruption of "phase sequences" that have been established by either perceptual experience or experimental training.

This paper has already suggested a way of applying the same general paradigm to the experimental study of motivation possibly produced by conflict.

Motivation for achievement. Observations of human and animal behavior suggest many additional possible sources of motivation for experimental study. For example, a child that has just learned to turn over from its stomach to its back may cry until it is placed on its stomach so that it can practice this fascinating act again. Can trial-and-error learning be motivated by this "drive"?

After the child has become skillful in turning over in both directions, he seems to become bored with this activity but strives persistently against many difficulties for other skills—to pull himself up, to stand, to walk, and eventually to ski. What is the drive and reward for each of these skills? Is there a separate drive for every maturing potential skill or is there some mechanism to produce in infants what might be loosely labeled as a general drive toward achievement? If so, what kind of mechanism could possibly produce this result? How much of the adult motive is attributable to rewards that channel such a drive and how much to some drive that is elicited by social punishments for failure to improve and rewards for improving?

Conceivably, the blocking of almost any response tends to induce motivation and the partial or complete occurrence of the blocked response tends to relieve the motivation and function as a reward. This hypothesis might be checked by eliciting movements, such as circling, by central stimulation and determining whether such stimulation can motivate learning without any additional rewards, if, and only if, the movements are first blocked and then released. It is just barely conceivable that such a mechanism might be one step toward the development of a motivation that would have some of the functions of a drive to achieve.

Certain ideas as motivation. Similarly, observation of infants strongly suggests that they have something like definite ideas and that these can serve as transient but strong motivations. I have observed a child under the age of nine months seem to get the idea that he wanted to get a certain tray off a low shelf, struggle vigorously this way and that until he finally succeeded, and then show a look of joy and triumph.

In the adult it is obvious that, as the definite result of social training, certain thoughts, such as "I may have cancer," can elicit strong motivation. I have described such motives as *mediated learned drives* [64]. Could this mechanism have been involved in the infant, and if so, how, or was some more basic mechanism involved, and if so, what?

Perhaps, as I have suggested in a discussion of *goal-directed drives* [64], the discrepancy between an anticipatory goal response (or certain other ideas) and the current state of affairs can be the basis for motivation. Again, we need to know far more empirical facts aimed at a penetrating analysis of the details of such behavior and its possible mechanisms.

Possible response characteristics in infant hunger. Let me conclude with one more concrete example. I have observed an infant during the first two weeks of life change within a few minutes from a state of relative quiescence to one of crying, reddening, and extreme activation so that my first reaction was to search for a jabbing pin. No such obvious source of activation was found, but when given a bottle, he drank vigorously and quieted down. If the milk in the bottle ran out, he became extremely activated, but by the time a new bottle could be heated, he sometimes had quieted down, was out of the mood, and refused it.

The suddenness of these shifts contrasts with what might be expected from the gradual accumulation (or restoration) of a physiological deficit; it suggests that hunger may have some of the properties of a response, being inhibited until it finally breaks through and then strengthens and maintains itself by positive feedback. On the other hand, perhaps it is not the hunger itself, but only the anticipatory goal responses or overt responses to the hunger, that have this characteristic.

In any event, it should be reasonably straightforward and profitable to devise objective techniques for recording the reactions of human or animal infants to hunger. Then one could systematically study the effects of a few simple controlled experimental operations of the type that frequently occur by chance in the natural environment.

Additional problems. In conclusion, let me emphasize that the foregoing examples are but a small sample of the types of naturalistic observations which point up the shortcomings of our current understanding of motivation. Each such observation could serve as the point of departure for a new line of research. I have made a number of suggestions, but these are meant more to point up the problems than to serve as definitive solutions to them. Many other problems remain to be raised. For example, some motivations in some people seem to be relatively central in that they cannot be changed without a profound effect on the entire personality; others are peripheral and can be changed with little effect. What are the principles and conditions that cause different motivations to be central with different individuals? Why are some learned drives amazingly resistant to change, whereas others change easily? How are hierarchies of learned drives and rewards built up, and how do they interact?